Management and Cost Accounting

Third Edition

Charles T. Horngren
Alnoor Bhimani
Srikant M. Datar
George Foster

Supplement

PROFESSIONAL EXAM QUESTIONS FROM

PAST *ACCA*, *CIMA*, AND *ICAI* PAPERS

with selected answers

Compiled by
Kamran Malik

Prentice Hall
FINANCIAL TIMES

An imprint of Pearson Education
Harlow, England • London • New York • Boston • San Francisco • Toronto
Sydney • Tokyo • Singapore • Hong Kong • Seoul • Taipei • New Delhi
Cape Town • Madrid • Mexico City • Amsterdam • Munich • Paris • Milan

Pearson Education Limited
Edinburgh Gate
Harlow
Essex CM20 2JE
England

and Associated Companies throughout the world.

Visit us on the World Wide Web at:
www.pearsoned.co.uk

First published 2002
Third edition published 2005

ISBN 0 273 68756 5

10 9 8 7 6 5 4 3 2 1

09   08   07   06   05

Printed in Great Britain

Introduction

This booklet contains 40 questions from past ACCA, CIMA and ICAI papers, plus suggested answers to selected questions.

Answers to a quarter of the questions are included in this booklet, allowing students to test their understanding of key topics and prepare for exams.

The answers to the remaining questions are available on the password-protected lecturer side of the companion website that supports this book at:

www.pearsoned.co.uk/horngren

This allows tutors to set selected questions for assignments and seminar use.

Acknowledgements

Our thanks to Kamran Malik for selecting the questions and sourcing the answers.

We are grateful to the following for permission to reproduce examination questions: Association of Chartered Certified Accountants (ACCA); Institute of Chartered Accountants in Ireland (ICAI); and Chartered Institute of Management Accountants (CIMA). The copyright of the questions belongs to ACCA, ICAI or CIMA and permission to reproduce these questions should be directed to the appropriate organisation. The examination boards are not responsible for the suggested answers to questions. All suggested answers have been provided by the author.

Companion Website and Instructor resources

Visit **www.pearsoned.co.uk/horngren** to find valuable online resources

For students

- Learning objectives for each chapter
- A mix of multiple choice, fill in the blank and true/false questions to help test your learning
- Annotated links to relevant sites on the web
- An online glossary to explain key terms

For instructors

- Complete, downloadable Instructor's Manual with teaching ideas and solutions to professional questions from the main text
- Suggested solutions to all case study material
- Editable PowerPoint slides and Overhead Projector Masters
- Solutions to additional questions and spreadsheet problems

Also: The Companion Website provides the following features:

- Search tool to help locate specific items of content
- E-mail results and profile tools to send results of quizzes to instructors
- Online help and support to assist with website usage and troubleshooting

For more information please contact your local Pearson Education sales representative or visit **www.pearsoned.co.uk/horngren**

OneKey: All you and your students need to succeed

OneKey is an exclusive new resource for instructors and students, giving you access to the best online teaching and learning tools 24 hours a day, 7 days a week.

OneKey means all your resources are in one place for maximum convenience, simplicity and success.

A OneKey product is available for *Management and Cost Accounting, third edition* for use with Blackboard™, WebCT and CourseCompass. It contains:

- Additional question material with spreadsheet problems
- Flashcards to test knowledge of key terms
- Additional case studies to illustrate management accounting in practice
- Extra professional questions to help consolidate understanding
- Video material with additional commentary about core topics

For more information about the OneKey product please contact your local Pearson Education sales representative or visit **www.pearsoned.co.uk/onekey**

Contents

The table below explains which solution pertains to which question paper. Answers not shown are on the website.

1

Question 1 – June 1999, ACCA

The Independent Film Company plc is a film distribution company which purchases distribution rights on films from small independent producers, and sells the films on to cinema chains for national and international screening. In recent years the company has found it difficult to source sufficient films to maintain profitability. In response to the problem, the Independent Film Company has decided to invest in commissioning and producing films in its own right. In order to gain the expertise for this venture, the Independent Film Company is considering purchasing an existing filmmaking concern, at a cost of £400,000.

The main difficulty that is anticipated for the business is the increasing uncertainty as to the potential success/failure rate of independently produced films. Many cinema chains are adopting a policy of only buying films from large international film companies, as they believe that the market for Independent films is very limited and specialist in nature. The Independent Film Company is prepared for the fact that they are likely to have more films that fail than that succeed, but believe that the proposed film production business will nonetheless be profitable.

Using data collected from the existing distribution business and discussions with industry experts, they have produced cost and revenue forecasts for the five years of operation of the proposed investment. The company aims to complete the production of three films per year. The after-tax cost of capital for the company is estimated to be 14%.

Year 1 sales for the new business are uncertain, but expected to be in the range of £4m–£10m.

Sales (£m)	Prob
4	0.2
5	0.4
7	0.3
10	0.1

Probability estimates for different forecast values are as follows:

Sales are expected to grow at an annual rate of 5%.
Anticipated costs related to the new business are as follows:

Cost Type	£'000
Purchase of film-making company	400
Annual legal and professional costs	20
Annual lease rental (office equipment)	12
Studio and set hire (per film)	180
Camera/specialist equipment hire (per film)	40
Technical staff wages (per film)	520
Screenplay (per film)	50
Actors' salaries (per film)	700

Costumes and wardrobe hire (per film)	60
Set design and painting (per film)	150
Annual non-production staff wages	60

Additional Information

(i)   No capital allowances are available.

(ii) Tax is payable one year in arrears, at a rate of 33% and full use can be made of tax refunds as they fall due.

(iii) Staff wages (technical and non-production staff) and actors' salaries, are expected to rise by 10% per annum.

(iv) Studio hire costs will be subject to an increase of 30% in Year 3.

(v)   Screenplay costs per film are expected to rise by 15% per annum due to a shortage of skilled writers.

(vi) The new business will occupy office accommodation which has to date been let out for an annual rent of £20,000. Demand for such accommodation is buoyant and the company anticipates no problems in finding future tenants at the same annual rent.

(vii) A market research survey into the potential for the film production business cost £25,000.

Required:

(a) Using DCF analysis, calculate the expected Net Present Value of the proposed investment. (Workings should be rounded to the nearest £'000.) **(15 marks)**

(b) Outline the main limitations of using expected values when making investment decisions. **(6 marks)**

(c) In addition to the possible purchase of the film-making business, the company has two other investment opportunities, the details of which are given below:

Post-Tax Cash Flows, £'000

	Year 0	Year 1	Year 2	Year 3	Year 4	Year 5	Year 6
Investment X	(200)	200	200	150	100	100	100
Investment Y	(100)	80	80	40	40	40	40

The Independent Film Company has a total of £400,000 available for capital investment in the current year. No project can be invested in more than once.

Required:

(i)   Define the term profitability index, and briefly explain how it may be used when a company faces a problem of capital rationing in any single accounting period. **(4 marks)**

(ii) Calculate the profitability index for each of the investment projects available to the Independent Film Company, i.e. purchase of the film production company, Investment X and Investment Y, and outline the optimal investment strategy. Assume that all of the projects are indivisible. **(6 marks)**

(iii) Explain the limitations of using a profitability index in a situation where there is capital rationing. **(4 marks)**

Management & Cost Accounting: Professional Exam Questions. © Pearson Education Limited 2005

(d) Briefly explain how the tax treatment of capital purchases can affect an investment decision.

(5 marks)

(40 marks)

© ACCA

2

Question 5 – June 1999, ACCA

As a recently appointed assistant management accountant you are attending a monthly performance meeting. You have with you a statement of monthly actual costs, a summary of cost variances and other pieces of information you have managed to collect, as shown below:

	£
Actual cost of direct material purchased and used	62,700
Actual direct wages paid	97,350
Variable overheads incurred	19,500
Fixed overheads incurred	106,500

The variances from standard cost were:

Direct Material Price Variance	5,700 Adv.
Direct Material Usage Variance	3,000 Fav.
Direct Labour Rate Variance	1,650 Fav.
Direct Labour Efficiency Variance	9,000 Fav.
Variable Overhead Variance	1,500 Adv.
Fixed Overhead Expenditure Variance	1,500 Adv.
Fixed Overhead Volume Variance	15,000 Adv.

The actual wage rate paid for the period was £8·85 per hour. It takes three standard hours to produce one unit of the finished product. The single direct material used in the period cost 30p per kg above the standard price. Five kg of raw material input is allowed for as standard for one unit of output.

All figures relate to the single product which is manufactured at the plant. There were no stocks at the beginning or end of the accounting period. Variable and fixed overhead absorption rates are based on standard hours produced. Managers from various functions have brought to the meeting measures which they have collected for their own areas of responsibility. In order to demonstrate the link between the accounting values and their measures you decide to work from the variances to confirm some of them.

Required:

(a) The formula for the calculation of the labour cost variance is: $(SH \times SR) - (AH \times AR)$
 Provide formulae for the calculation of the labour rate variance and labour efficiency variance using similar notation to that above. Demonstrate how they will sum to the labour cost variance given above.
 (2 marks)

(b) Using variance formulae, such as those above, or otherwise, determine:
 (i)   the actual number of direct labour hours worked
 (ii) the standard rate of pay per direct labour hour
 (iii) the standard hours of production
 (iv) the actual production in units
 (v)   the actual quantity of direct material consumed

Management & Cost Accounting: Professional Exam Questions. © Pearson Education Limited 2005

(vi) the actual price paid for the direct material (per kg)

(vii) the standard direct material usage in kg for the actual number of units produced.

(10 marks)

(c) From (b) above and any other calculations which may be appropriate, compute the standard cost per unit of finished product. Show separately standard prices and standard quantities for each element of cost. (4 marks)

(d) Briefly interpret the overhead variances given in the question. (4 marks)

(20 marks)

© ACCA

Question 1 – June 2000, ACCA Paper B2

Anson Limited manufactures a single product, Product X, in two successive processes. The following information relates to the month of April 2000:

	Process 1	**Process 2**
Opening Work-in-Progress	Nil	Nil
Materials input during month	500 units at a cost of £10,250	400 units from Process 1
Additional materials	———	£11,300
Labour cost for month	£33,000	£14,280
Production overhead cost for month	£18,040	£ 8,120
Normal loss	Nil	50 units
Transferred to Process 2	400 units	
Transferred to Finished Goods stock	———	350 units
Closing Work-in-Progress	100 units 100% complete for materials and 40% complete for conversion costs	Nil

Note: The normal loss in Process 2 was detected at the end of the process, and was sold as scrap for £800 and was credited to Process 2. There was no abnormal loss in either process.

Required:

(a) For the month of April 2000 produce separately each of Process 1 and Process 2 ledger accounts. Your accounts should clearly show the values of goods transferred between processes and to finished goods stock and the value of work-in-progress. The accounts should also clearly show 'units' as well as values. (17 marks)

(b) Product X is sold for £350 per unit. It is possible to convert Product X into Product Y by way of a further process. The total cost of conversion would be £38 per unit input, but there would be a normal loss of 20% of input. Product Y could be sold for £450 per unit. Calculate the effect on the total profit of Anson Limited if it decided to convert the total production of Product X into Product Y. (8 marks)

(25 marks)

© ACCA

4

Question 6 – June 1999, ACCA

A holiday company offers a range of package holidays abroad. The management are examining the viability of three types of holiday for the coming season.

An analysis of costs and revenues of each of the holiday packages is shown below:

	£	Sports Holiday 100 £	£	Culture Holiday 100 £	£	Special Interest Holiday 100 £
Maximum Number of Customers						
Total Revenue (100 customers)		42,000		48,000		30,000
Costs: (100 customers)						
Air Travel	8,100		8,400		7,800	
Hotel and Meals	16,800		19,800		7,200	
Local Courier	1,500		1,500		1,750	
Other customer costs and office overheads	10,560		11,880		6,180	
Commission	6,300		4,800		6,000	
		43,260		46,380		28,930
Profit/(Loss)		£ (1,260)		£1,620		£1,070

Past experience has shown that the average number of places taken up on the holidays, as a percentage of the maximum number of customers, will be 70% on sports, 80% on culture and 60% on special interest holidays.

The costs of the local couriers will not change irrespective of the number of customers. The costs of air travel are also fixed and are based on a block booking of seats for the season. The booking with the airline has already been confirmed. Contracts for the couriers have not yet been signed. All accommodation costs are variable with the number of passengers. The commission is proportional to the price of the holiday.

The other customer costs and office overheads, in the table above, are allocated over all the company's different package holidays. They are semi-variable costs and an analysis of these costs for the last three years relating to all holidays is as follows:

	Total number of customers	Total customer costs and office overheads £
1996	10,000	900,000
1997	12,000	990,000
1998	15,000	1,125,000

The effects of exchange rates and inflation may be ignored.

Required:

(a) Analyse the costs and revenues into a form more suitable to an assessment of the short-term viability of each holiday. Calculate one possible break-even number of customers required for each holiday.

N.B. Your analysis should be presented showing, where appropriate, costs and revenues per customer. (10 marks)

(b) Identify clearly the shortcomings of the original analysis, explain your preferred analysis and interpret the results. (10 marks)

(20 marks)

© ACCA

5

Question 1 – 2002, ACCA Pilot Paper

Brandwell Limited makes three products from a single process. During September 2001, the inputs into the process were:

> direct materials – 1,000 kilograms at a total cost of £5,500
> direct labour – £6,500
> factory overheads – £7,000

There is a normal loss in process of 10%.

The 900 kilograms output from the process in September 2001 was as follows:

> Product X: 50%
> Product Y: 40%
> Product Z: 10%

Selling prices for the products are:

> Product X: £30·00 per kilogram
> Product Y: £18·75 per kilogram
> Product Z: £25·00 per kilogram

Required:

Calculate separately, for September 2001, the joint costs to be apportioned to each of Products X, Y and Z based on:

(a) the relative or proportional weight of output, and   (6 marks)

(b) the relative revenue arising from the sale of each product.   (9 marks)

                                                             (15 marks)

© ACCA

6

Question 2 – December 1999, ACCA Paper B2

Foxfield plc manufactures three types of bottles, Q1, Q2 and Q3. The following information relates to the standard raw material used to make each type of bottle.

Bottle type	Q1	Q2	Q3
Material	300 grammes	400 grammes	500 grammes

The standard cost of raw material is £0.30 per kilogramme and the bottles are always produced in the ratio of 4:3:1.

Total production quantities can vary from week to week. Company records show that in the last year the highest weekly production level achieved was 16,000 bottles and the lowest weekly production level was just 12,800 bottles.

The company employs a total of 10 production staff, each of whom is paid £140 per week, whatever production level is achieved. The number of staff that work on each type of bottle is as follows:

Bottle type	Q1	Q2	Q3
Employees	4	4	2

Production overheads are all fixed costs and total £5,400 per week. They are apportioned to each type of bottle in the ratio of 4:3:2.

Required:

(a) Calculate how many bottles of each type were produced in the week with the highest production level and how many bottles of each type were produced in the week with the lowest production level.   (2 marks)

(b) Calculate separately the cost of producing a single unit of each type of bottle when the weekly production level achieved is:
  (i)   12,800 bottles in total
  (ii) 16,000 bottles in total.
  Calculate the unit costs to four decimal places of a £.   (17 marks)

(c) Completed bottles are sent to another company for cleaning, labelling and packing. This company employs several part-time personnel to clean, label and pack the bottles. These staff are paid on an incremental piecework basis. The details of the piecework scheme are as follows:

No of bottles prepared and packed	Rate paid per bottle
1 – 2,000	1.6p
2,001 – 3,000	1.7p
3,001 – 4,000	1.8p

* Note: Only the extra bottles qualify for the higher rates, and any bottles that are broken are deducted from the number of bottles that qualify for piecework.

The figures below refer to the output achieved by three of the employees during a recent week:

Employee	A	B	C
Bottles prepared and packed	2,500	3,200	3,900
Bottles broken	50	150	100

Calculate separately the amount payable to each of employees A, B and C based on the output achieved above.   (6 marks)

(25 marks)

© ACCA

7

Question 2 – December 1999, ACCA

Benland plc manufacture and fit a variety of children's playground equipment. The company at present purchases the rubber particles used in the playground surfacing from an outside supplier, but is considering investing in equipment which would process and shred used vehicle tyres to produce equivalent rubber particles. One tonne of purchased particles is saved per tonne of tyres processed. Disposal of used tyres is becoming an environmental problem, and Benland believes that it could charge £40 per tonne to garages/tyre distributors wishing to dispose of their old tyres. This price would be 20 per cent lower than the cost of the landfill sites currently being used, and so Benland believes that it would face no risk or shortage of supply of what would be a key raw material for the business. The price charged by Benland for tyre disposal (£40 per tonne) remains fixed for the next five years.

The cost to Benland of purchased particles is £3·50 per tonne for each of the next five years, and the price has been contractually guaranteed. If the contract is terminated within the next two years, Benland will be charged an immediate termination penalty of £100,000 which will not be allowed as a tax deductible expense. The machine required to process the tyres will cost £1·06 million, and it is estimated that at the end of year five the machine will have a second-hand value of £120,000 before selling costs of £5,000.

Sales of the playground surfacing which uses rubber particles are forecast to be £1·2 million in year one, rising by 10% per year until year five but prices will remain constant.

The new equipment will result in Benland incurring additional maintenance costs of £43,000 per year. 80,000 tonnes of tyres need to be processed in order to meet the raw material requirement for the forecast sales in year one.

Processing costs are estimated at £37 per tonne (excluding additional depreciation and maintenance).

Benland is subject to corporation tax at a rate of 33%, payable one year in arrears. Capital expenditure is eligible for 25% allowances on a reducing balance basis, and sales proceeds of assets are subject to tax.

Benland has sufficient profits to fully utilise all available capital allowances.

Required:

(a) Using 12% as the after-tax discount rate, advise Benland on the desirability of purchasing the tyre processing equipment.   (12 marks)

(b) Discuss which cash flows are most important in determining the outcome of the proposed investment and how Benland might seek to minimise the risk of large changes in predicted cash flows.   (8 marks)

(20 marks)

© ACCA

8

Question from Autumn 1996, ICAI

Some managements flex a budget linearly when wishing to make the budgeted volume and actual volume production more comparable. The basis for flexing can be either labour-hours or machine-hours.

Required:

1   Discuss why flexing a budget linearly on the basis of either labour-hours or machine-hours may not be an appropriate basis.   (9 marks)

2   Discuss how flexing a budget on a labour- or machine-hours basis may reduce effective cost control.   (5 marks)

3   Discuss an alternative method of budgeting which might increase the relevance of the budget and improve effective cost control.   (6 marks)

(Total marks = 20)

© ICAI

9

Question from Summer 1995, ICAI

(a) A management accountant might refer to the following types of standards. What do you think they refer to?
  (i) Basic standards
  (ii) Ideal standards
  (iii) Currently attainable standards. (8 marks)

(b) FERRA Ltd has developed the following standard for one of its products – the LOOM:
Standard – 1 unit of LOOM

		£
Materials:	10 kg of Y @ £4.50 per kg	45
Labour:	4 hours @ £6 per hour	24
Variable overheads:	4 hours @ £4.50 per hour	18
		87

Budgeted fixed overhead for Period 2 is £12 500.

The following information is available in respect of Period 2.

Actual output was 8250 units of LOOM. Actual costs were as follows:

Materials purchases:	96 500 kg of Y costing £437 980
Materials usage:	86 450 kg of Y
Labour:	Wages – £196 800 for 32 000 hours of direct labour
Variable overheads:	£136 000
Fixed overheads:	£11 750

Required:

Calculate each of the following variances for LOOM for Period 2.
(i) Materials price and usage variances. (4 marks)

(ii) Labour rate and efficiency variances. (3 marks)

(iii) Variable overhead expenditure and efficiency variances. (3 marks)

(iv) Fixed overhead expenditure variance. (2 marks)

(Total marks = 20)

© ICAI

10

Question 5 – December 1999, ACCA

A small company is engaged in the production of plastic tools for the garden.

Sub-totals on the spreadsheet of budgeted overheads for a year reveal:

	Moulding Department	Finishing Department	General Factory Overhead
Variable overhead £000	1,600	500	1,050
Fixed overhead £000	2,500	850	1,750
Budgeted activity Machine hours (000)	800	600	
Practical capacity Machine hours (000)	1,200	800	

For the purposes of reallocation of general factory overhead it is agreed that the variable overheads accrue in line with the machine hours worked in each department. General factory fixed overhead is to be reallocated on the basis of the practical machine hour capacity of the two departments.

It has been a long-standing company practice to establish selling prices by applying a mark-up on full manufacturing cost of between 25% and 35%.

A possible price is sought for one new product which is in a final development stage. The total market for this product is estimated at 200,000 units per annum. Market research indicates that the company could expect to obtain and hold about 10% of the market. It is hoped the product will offer some improvement over competitors' products, which are currently marketed at between £90 and £100 each.

The product development department have determined that the direct material content is £9 per unit. Each unit of the product will take two labour hours (four machine hours) in the moulding department and three labour hours (three machine hours) in finishing. Hourly labour rates are £5·00 and £5·50 respectively.

Management estimate that the annual fixed costs which would be specifically incurred in relation to the product are: supervision £20,000, depreciation of a recently acquired machine £120,000 and advertising £27,000. It may be assumed that these costs are included in the budget given above. Given the state of development of this new product, management do not consider it necessary to make revisions to the budgeted actvity levels given above for any possible extra machine hours involved in its manufacture.

Required:

(a) Briefly explain the role of costs in pricing. (6 marks)

(b) Prepare full cost and marginal cost information which may help with the pricing decision.

(9 marks)

(c) Comment on the cost information and suggest a price range which should be considered.

(5 marks)

(20 marks)

© ACCA

Question 2 – 2002, ACCA Pilot Paper

Redgate Limited is a manufacturing company. The budgeted factory overheads for next year, ending on 31 December 2002, have already been apportioned as shown below:

		Production Departments		Service Departments	
	Total £	Cutting £	Assembly £	Storeroom £	Maintenance £
Apportioned overheads	340,000	210,000	80,000	22,000	28,000

The following information is also relevant:

	Cutting	Assembly	Storeroom	Maintenance
Material requisitions	140	60		20
Maintenance hours	210	90		
Machine hours	8,750	11,750		
Labour hours	7,000	19,000		

Required:

(a) Re-apportion the service department's overheads using an appropriate basis in each case.

(7 marks)

(b) Calculate overhead absorption rates for the production departments based on the information provided.   (8 marks)

(15 marks)

© ACCA

12

Question 3 – December 1999, ACCA Paper B2

Dataline Limited operates a computer bureau and provides four types of services to small business clients.

The services are:
– Data processing undertaken by the Data Input Department.
– Designing programs undertaken by the Programming Department.
– Supply of computer systems undertaken by the Installation Department.
– Maintenance and repair of computer systems undertaken by the Maintenance Department.

The labour and overhead costs for the company for the year to 31 December 2000 are expected to be as follows:

Dataline Limited
Forecast labour & overhead costs for the year to 31 Dec 2000

	£
Programmers' salaries	87,000
Installation Engineers' salaries (#)	74,200
Input clerks' salaries	56,000
Management salaries (*)	43,440
Rent and rates	88,000
Insurance of premises	22,000
Security services	17,600
Electricity costs	9,200
Depreciation of computer equipment	29,500
Depreciation of office equipment	10,200
	£437,140

(#) Installation Engineers' salaries are shared between the Maintenance Department and the Installation Department in proportion to the budgeted hours for those departments.

(*) Management salaries are apportioned to the other departments in proportion to the salaries of the other departments.

The following information is also available:

	Data Input	Programming	Installation	Maintenance
Value of Computer Equipment (£)	400,000	120,000	40,000	30,000
Value of Office Equipment (£)	30,000	10,000	15,000	5,000
Floor area (Square metres)	1,000	200	600	400
Electricity usage (Kilowatt hours)	2,800	1,000	400	400
Forecast operating hours	12,000	4,800	3,000	7,600

Required:

(a) Produce an overhead apportionment schedule for the year to 31 December 2000. (14 marks)

(b) Calculate separately an overhead absorption rate for:
   (i)   the Programming Department   (2 marks)
   (ii) the Maintenance Department   (2 marks)
   (iii) the Data Input Department, and   (2 marks)
   (iv) the Installation Department.   (2 marks)
   Calculation of overhead absorption rates should be to four decimal places.

(c) Assuming that the following hours were actually worked during the year ended 31 December 2000, and the following costs were actually incurred, calculate separately the amount of overhead over-absorbed or under-absorbed in each department. (4 marks)

	Data Input	Programming	Installation	Maintenance
Actual operating hours	13,000	4,900	2,400	7,100
Actual overheads incurred (£)	164,200	129,850	54,150	87,500

Answers should be given to the nearest £.

(d) Describe the book-keeping treatment of both over-absorbed and under-absorbed overhead in the cost accounting ledger. (2 marks)

(e) Activity-based costing is an alternative approach to finding the overhead cost per unit in absorption costing. Give two examples of cost drivers that could be used in activity-based costing and their associated costs. (2 marks)

(30 marks)

© ACCA

13

Question from Autumn 1996, ICAI

Meteor plc manufactures a product 'QX' with a standard unit selling price of £40.

	£	£
Sales price per unit		40.00
Direct material – 4 kg at £3 per kg	12.00	
Direct labour – 3 hours at £6 per hour	18.00	
		30.00
Contribution per unit		10.00

In Period 1, the budgeted output was 2000 units but the actual output was 2250 units, which were all sold at £40 per unit. The following information is available for Period 1.

The material used for producing product 'QX' was not available from the supplier due to a fire at the supplier's unit. Meteor plc had to purchase a substitute material from another source to maintain production and sales. The usage and price for the substitute material for Period 1 for one unit of product 'QX' was expected to be 2.50 kg at a price of £2.50 per kg. The actual usage of the substitute material in the period was 11 000 kg and the actual cost was £28 500. The substitute material required additional care by the labour force and consequently management agreed to increase the labour rate per hour to £6.50. During Period 1, the labour force was paid for 7000 hours.

Required:

1   Calculate the budgeted contribution from a 2250 unit base and reconcile it with the actual contribution in Period 1, using the conventional variances method.   (5 marks)

2   Discuss the use of planning and operational variances and how they differ from the conventional variance method.   (9 marks)

3   Calculate the planning and operational variances for material in Period 1 and compare them with the conventional material variances.   (6 marks)

(Total marks = 20)

© ICAI

14

Question 4 – June 2000, ACCA

A Public Sector Organisation is extending its budgetary control and responsibility accounting system to all departments. One such department concerned with public health and welfare is called 'Homecare'. The department consists of staff who visit elderly 'clients' in their homes to support them with their basic medical and welfare needs.

A monthly cost control report is to be sent to the department manager, a copy of which is also passed to a Director who controls a number of departments. In the system, which is still being refined, the budget was set by the Director and the manager had not been consulted over the budget or the use of the monthly control report.

Shown below is the first month's cost control report for the Homecare department.

Cost Control Report – Homecare Department
Month ending May 2000

	Budget	Actual	(Overspend)/ Underspend
Visits	10,000	12,000	(2,000)
	£	£	£
Department expenses:			
Supervisory salary	2,000	2,125	(125)
Wages (Permanent staff)	2,700	2,400	300
Wages (Casual staff)	1,500	2,500	(1,000)
Office equipment depreciation	500	750	(250)
Repairs to equipment	200	20	180
Travel expenses	1,500	1,800	(300)
Consumables	4,000	6,000	(2,000)
Administration and telephone	1,000	1,200	(200)
Allocated administrative costs	2,000	3,000	(1000)
	15,400	19,795	(4,395)

In addition to the manager and permanent members of staff, appropriately qualified casual staff are appointed on a week-to-week basis to cope with fluctuations in demand. Staff use their own transport and travel expenses are reimbursed. There is a central administration overhead charge over all departments. Consumables consist of materials which are used by staff to care for clients. Administration and telephone are costs of keeping in touch with the staff who often operate from their own homes.

As a result of the report, the Director sent a memo to the manager of the Homecare department pointing out that the department must spend within its funding allocation and that any spending more than 5% above budget on any item would not be tolerated. The Director requested an immediate explanation for the serious overspend.

You work as the assistant to the Directorate Management Accountant. On seeing the way the budget system was developing, he made a note of points he would wish to discuss and develop further, but was called away before these could be completed.

Required:

(a) Develop and explain the issues concerning the budgetary control and responsibility accounting system which are likely to be raised by the management accountant. You should refer to the way the budget was prepared, the implications of a 20% increase in the number of visits, the extent of controllability of costs, the implications of the funding allocation, social aspects and any other points you think appropriate. You may include numerical illustrations and comment on specific costs, but you are not required to reproduce the cost control report.   (14 marks)

(b) Briefly explain Zero-Based Budgeting (ZBB), describe how (in a situation such as that above) it might be implemented, and how as a result it could improve the budget setting procedure.
(6 marks)

(20 marks)

© ACCA

15

Question 3 – June 1999, ACCA Paper B2

Torwood Limited is planning to manufacture a compound X72 that will be used in the food industry. The product will be sold for £15.00 per kilo. The company expects the following standards to apply to the production of the compound.

> Ingredient M1: 0·25 kilos @ £2·00 per kilo
> Ingredient M2: 0·75 kilos @ £3·00 per kilo
> Labour: 0·20 hours @ £4·00 per hour
> Variable overhead is absorbed @ £6·00 per labour hour
> Fixed overheads are expected to be £6,600 per annum.
> They are absorbed on a unit basis and will accrue evenly over the year

The planned production and sales levels for the first 3 months of the year ending 31 December 2000 are expected to be:

Month	January	February	March
Production (units)	110	100	120
Sales (units)	80	110	100

The production levels in January to March are similar to the production levels that are planned for the other 3-month periods during the forthcoming year. The company had no stocks of raw materials or finished goods on 1 January 2000.

Required:

You are required to:

(a) Produce a detailed standard cost card for 1 kilo of product X72 using:
    (i)   absorption costing
    (ii) marginal costing   (6 marks)

(b) Produce a detailed forecast profit and loss account for the three month period ending on 31 March 2000 using;
    (i)   absorption costing
    (ii) marginal costing   (16 marks)

(c) Produce a statement reconciling the profit calculated in part (b)(i) with that calculated in part (b)(ii)   (3 marks)

(25 marks)

© ACCA

16

Question 3 – June 2000, ACCA Paper B2

Cascade Limited produces metal containers for the pharmaceutical industry. The company uses standard costing and the following standards relate to the containers:

Material: 6 kilos of Material A at £5·00 per kilo.
Direct labour: 2 hours at a rate of £4·50 per hour.
Variable overheads are absorbed at a rate of £7·50 per labour hour.
Fixed overheads are absorbed at a rate of £12·00 per labour hour and are budgeted at £15,000 per month.

During May 2000 the company produced and sold 600 containers. The actual costs and data relating to production in May were as follows:

Material: 3,550 kilos at a total cost of £18,290
Direct labour: 1,320 hours were worked and paid for at a total cost of £5,610
Variable overhead incurred was £9,400
Fixed overhead incurred was £15,610

Required:

(a) Calculate the standard cost of a single metal container.   (5 marks)

(b) Calculate the following cost variances for May 2000:
    (i)   Material price and usage;   (4 marks)
    (ii) Labour rate and efficiency;   (4 marks)
    (iii) Variable overhead expenditure (or rate) and efficiency;   (6 marks)
    (iv) Fixed overhead expenditure and volume.   (6 marks)

(25 marks)

© ACCA

17

Question from Autumn 1995, ICAI

The following operating statement for Lavender Ltd for the six months ended 30 June 1995 is to be considered at a management meeting of the Managing Director, Production Director and Management Accountant of the company.

Operating statement – six months ended 30 June 1995

	Budget units (000s)	Actual units (000s)	Variance units (000s)	
Sales	1 000	900	100	Adverse
Production	1 000	900	100	Adverse
	(£000s)	**(£000s)**	**(£000s)**	
Sales	11 000	9 650	1 350	Adverse
Direct materials	5 000	4 300	700	Favourable
Direct labour	2 000	1 700	300	Favourable
Variable production overhead	1 000	905	95	Favourable
Variable sales overhead	950	975	25	Adverse
Total variable costs	8 950	7 880	1 070	Favourable
Contribution	2 050	1 770	280	Adverse
Fixed production overhead	1 350	1 305	45	Favourable
Fixed selling overhead	200	265	65	Adverse
Total fixed overheads	1 550	1 570	20	Adverse
Profit	500	200	300	Adverse
	Hours (000s)	**Hours (000s)**	**Hours (000s)**	
Direct machine-hours	100	90	10	Adverse
Direct labour-hours	200	180	20	Adverse

The Production Director, who has received the statement for his information and attention, is concerned about the results shown therein. He and his staff feel that they have performed well during the six-month period. He would like to be able to argue this case at the meeting.

The Production Department produced all the production units ordered by the Sales Department. There were no opening or closing stocks. Variable production overhead is variable with direct labour.

Required:

1   Prepare a revised operating statement which more appropriately reflects the performance of the Production and Sales Departments for the period.   (9 marks)

2   Give all the production and sales variances.   (5 marks)

3   From the revised operating statement and production variances, prepare a short report for the Production Director, based on the relevant information, which would be useful to him in preparing himself for the management meeting.   (6 marks)

(Total marks = 20)

© ICAI

18

Question 3 – 2002, ACCA Pilot Paper

It is difficult for a company to identify the actual price paid for an individual item of material in stock. As a result a company can use a number of different methods for pricing materials issued to production.

Required:

(a) Give the names of three methods of pricing material issues.   (3 marks)

Broadvale Limited has budgeted to use 600 units of Material X during the year ending 31 December 2002. The material will be used during the year at an even rate. The material can be purchased in sizes of 100, 150, 200, 300 and 600.

The costs associated with the material are as follows:

Ordering costs = £10 per order
Holding costs = £0·50 per unit per year

Required:

(b) Calculate the values for each of the items in the table below labelled (t) to (z).

Order Size	No of orders	Ordering	Holding	Total cost
100	6	60·00	(u)	185·00
150	4	40·00	(v)	(z)
200	3	30·00	(w)	180·00
300	2	20·00	(x)	195·00
600	1	(t)	(y)	160·00

(7 marks)

(c) The economic order quantity (EOQ) formula is given as:

$$\sqrt{(2Cod \div Ch)}$$

where Co = ordering costs, d = annual demand and Ch = holding costs per unit per year.

Required:

Using the formula, calculate the economic order quantity for Material X for the year ending 31 December 2002.   (5 marks)

(15 marks)

© ACCA

19

Question from Stage 1, May 1995, CIMA

The Management Service Division of a company has been asked to evaluate the following proposals for the maintenance of a new boiler with a life of seven years:

Proposal 1. The boiler supplier will make a charge of £13,000 per year on a seven-year contract.

Proposal 2. The company will carry out its own maintenance estimated at £10,000 per annum now, rising at 5% per annum with a major overhaul at the end of year 4 costing an additional £25,000.

The discount rate is 10% and all payments are assumed to be made at year ends.

Required:

1   Calculate the maintenance cost for each year if the company provides its own maintenance.

(4 marks)

2   Calculate the present value of the cost of maintenance, if the company carries out its own maintenance.

(4 marks)

3   Calculate the present value of the supplier's maintenance contract.   (3 marks)

4   Recommend, with reasons, which proposal should be adopted.   (4 marks)

Total = (15 marks)

© CIMA

20

Question 4 – 2002, ACCA Pilot Paper

Entity Limited is a manufacturer of a component for the motor industry. The standard cost card for the component is shown below:

		£
Direct materials	5 kilograms at £5·00 per kilogram	25
Direct labour	2 hours at £4·00 per hour	8
Variable factory overhead	£2·00 per direct labour hour	4
Fixed factory overhead	£5·50 per direct labour hour	<u>11</u>
Total standard cost		48

Actual production for the month ended 31 October 2001 was 200 units and the actual costs incurred were:

Direct materials	900 kilograms at a total cost of £5,400
Direct labour	420 hours at a total cost of £1,638
Variable factory overheads	£780
Fixed factory overheads	£2,300

Required:

(a) Calculate the standard selling price of a component if the company requires a standard profit equal to 25% of the selling price. (2 marks)

(b) Calculate the following variances for the month of October 2001:
  (i)   material price (1 mark)
  (ii) material usage (1 mark)
  (iii) labour rate (1 mark)
  (iv) labour efficiency (1 mark)
  (v)   variable overhead expenditure (1 mark)
  (vi) variable overhead efficiency (2 marks)
  (vii) total fixed overhead. (2 marks)

(c) Give two reasons for each of the following variances:
  (i)   material price (2 marks)
  (ii) labour rate. (2 marks)

(15 marks)

© ACCA

21

Question from June 1997, ACCA

The Alphab Group has five divisions, A, B, C, D and E. Group management wish to increase overall group production capacity per year by up to 30 000 hours. Part of the strategy will be to require that the minimum increase at any one division must be equal to 5% of its current capacity. The maximum funds available for the expansion programme are £3 000 000.

Additional information relating to each division is as follows:

Division	Existing capacity (hours)	Investment cost per hour (£)	Average contribution per hour (£)
A	20 000	90	12.50
B	40 000	75	9.50
C	24 000	100	11.00
D	50 000	120	8.00
E	12 000	200	14.00

A linear programme of the plan has been prepared in order to determine the strategy which will maximise additional contribution per annum and to provide additional decision-making information. Appendix I (below) shows a printout of the LP model of the situation.

Required:

(a) Formulate the mathematical model from which the input to the LP programme would be obtained.

(b) Use the linear programme solution in Appendix I in order to answer the following:

    (i) State the maximum additional contribution from the expansion strategy and the distribution of the extra capacity between the divisions.   (3 marks)

    (ii) Explain the cost to the company of providing the minimum 5% increase in capacity at each division.   (3 marks)

    (iii) Explain the effect on contribution of the limits placed on capacity and investment.

    (2 marks)

    (iv) Explain the sensitivity of the plan to changes in contribution per hour.   (4 marks)

APPENDIX I
Divisional investment evaluation
Optimal solution – detailed report

	Variable	Value
1	DIV A	22 090.91
2	DIV B	2 000.00
3	DIV C	1 200.00
4	DIV D	2 500.00
5	DIV E	2 209.09

	Constraint	Type	RHS*	Slack	Shadow price
1	Max. Hours	≤	30 000.00	0.00	11.2727
2	DIV A	≥	1 000.00	21090.91	0.0000
3	DIV B	≥	2 000.00	0.00	– 2.7955
4	DIV C	≥	1 200.00	0.00	–1.6364
5	DIV D	≥	2 500.00	0.00	–4.9091
6	DIV E	≥	600.00	1609.09	0.0000
7	Max. Funds	≤	3 000 000.00	0.00	0.0136

Objective function value = 359 263.6

Sensitivity analysis of objective function coefficients

Variable	Current coefficient	Allowable minimum	Allowable maximum
1 DIV A	12.50	10.7000	14.0000
2 DIV B	9.50	infinity	12.2955
3 DIV C	11.00	infinity	12.6364
4 DIV D	8.00	infinity	12.9091
5 DIV E	14.00	12.5000	27.7778

Sensitivity analysis of right-hand side values

	Constraint	Type	Current value	Allowance minimum	Allowance maximum
1	Max. Hours	≤	30 000.00	18 400.00	31 966.67
2	DIV A	≥	1 000.00	infinity	22 090.91
3	DIV B	≥	2 000.00	0.00	20 560.00
4	DIV C	≥	1 200.00	0.00	18 900.00
5	DIV D	≥	2 500.00	0.00	8 400.00
6	DIV E	≥	600.00	infinity	2 209.09
7	Max. Funds	≤	3 000 000.00	2 823 000.00	5 320 000.00

*RHS = Right-hand side

(v) Group management decide to relax the 30 000 hours capacity constraint. All other parameters of the model remain unchanged. Determine the change in strategy which will then maximise the increase in group contribution. You should calculate the increase in contribution which this change in strategy will provide. (6 marks)

(vi) Group management wish to decrease the level of investment while leaving all other parameters of the model (as per Appendix I) unchanged. Determine and quantify the change in strategy which is required indicating the fall in contribution which will occur. (6 marks)

(c) Explain the limitations of the use of linear programming for planning purposes. (5 marks)

(Total marks = 29 marks)

© ACCA

Question 2 – November 2001, CIMA FMAF

SS Ltd makes and sells a single product "PP". The company uses a standard absorption costing system.

The budgeted production and sales for the year ended 31 October 2001 were 59,500 units with a selling price of £2 each unit. The standard time for producing each unit was 3 minutes. The standard labour rate was £10 an hour. The standard material cost for one unit of PP was £0.75 per unit.

Production overhead absorption rates were based on direct labour cost and were as follows:

Variable overhead	35% of direct labour cost
Fixed overhead	40% of direct labour cost

For the year under review, the actual results were as follows:

Production and sales of PP	62,000 units
	£
Selling price for one unit	2.00
Labour cost incurred – for 3,500 hours	38,500
Material cost for each unit	0.75
Variable production overhead incurred	9,500
Fixed production overhead incurred	9,500

There were no changes in any stock levels during the period.

Required:

(a) Prepare a statement that reconciles budgeted profit with actual profit for the year ended 31 October 2001, showing the analysis of variances in as much detail as possible from the information given.   *(14 marks)*

(a) Referring to your analysis in part *(a)*, suggest two possible reasons for the labour efficiency variance and two possible reasons for the labour rate variance that you have calculated.   *(4 marks)*

(c) Explain the factors that should be considered when selecting the most appropriate base to use for an overhead absorption rate. Your answer should include a discussion of the method used by SS Ltd.   *(7 marks)*

(Total = 25 marks)

© CIMA

23

Question 3 – November 2001, CIMA FMAF

T Ltd is a newly-formed company that designs customised computer programs for its clients. The capital needed to fund the company will be provided by a venture capitalist who will invest £150,000 on 1 January 2002 in exchange for shares in T Ltd.

The Directors are currently gathering the information needed to help in the preparation of the cash budget for the first three months of 2002. The information that they have is given below.

Budget details
The budgeted sales (that is, the value of the contracts signed) for the first quarter of 2002 are expected to be £200,000. However, as the company will only just have commenced trading, it is thought that sales will need time to grow. It is therefore expected that 15% of the first quarter's sales will be achieved in January, 30% in February and the remainder in March. It is expected that sales for the year ending 31 December 2002 will reach £1,000,000.

Clients must pay a deposit of 5% of the value of the computer program when they sign the contract for the program to be designed. Payments of 45% and 50% of the value are then paid one and two months later respectively. No bad debts are anticipated in the first quarter.

There are six people employed by the company, each earning an annual gross salary of £45,000, payable in arrears on the last day of each month.

Computer hardware and software will be purchased for £100,000 in January. A deposit of 25% is payable on placing the order for the computer hardware and software, with the remaining balance being paid in equal amounts in February and March. The capital outlay will be depreciated on a straight-line basis over three years, assuming no residual value.

The company has decided to rent offices that will require an initial deposit of £13,000 and an ongoing cost of £6,500 per month payable in advance. These offices are fully serviced and the rent is inclusive of all fixed overhead costs.

Variable production costs are paid in the month in which they are incurred and are budgeted as follows:

<blockquote>

January £1,200 *February* £4,200 *March* £8,000

</blockquote>

A marketing and advertising campaign will be launched in January at a cost of £10,000 with a further campaign in March for £5,000, both amounts being payable as they are incurred.

Administration overhead is budgeted to be £500 each month: 60% to be paid in the month of usage and the balance one month later.

Tax and interest charges can be ignored.

Management & Cost Accounting: Professional Exam Questions. © Pearson Education Limited 2005

Required:

(a) Prepare the cash budget by month and in total for the first quarter of 2002. *(15 marks)*

(b) Identify and comment on those areas of the cash budget that you wish to draw to the attention of the Directors of T Ltd, and recommend action to improve cash flow. *(7 marks)*

(c) Briefly explain three advantages for T Ltd of using a spreadsheet when preparing a cash budget. *(3 marks)*

(Total = 25 marks)

© CIMA

24

Question 4 – May 2001, CIMA FMAF

A medical practice had some unused space which it decided to use to expand the services provided to the local community. It has established a new specialist unit, which offers general health assessments and medical assessments for patients. The general health assessment involves a trained nurse assessing a patient's general health and if, for any reason, a patient requires a medical assessment, the nurse refers them to a doctor.

It is estimated that the standard times are 30 minutes for a general health assessment by the nurse, and an additional 60 minutes for a medical assessment by a doctor. The nurse and the doctor work independently of each other.

The medical practice employs the nurse and the doctor on a subcontract basis. The standard labour rates are as follows:

Nurse	£12 per hour
Doctor	£30 per hour

A total of 2,000 general health assessments and 250 medical assessments are budgeted for the forthcoming period.

Fixed overheads for the specialist unit are budgeted at £20,000 for the forthcoming period. These overheads are to be absorbed on an assessment-hour basis.

Although the medical practice is a non-profit making organisation, it is concerned that costs are controlled and that it offers a high-quality service.

Actual results:

The following actual results were recorded for the period:

The nurse carried out 2,200 general health assessments and was paid £22,500 for working 1,500 hours.

The doctor carried out 300 medical assessments and was paid £9,800 for working 350 hours.

The fixed overheads amounted to £22,000.

Required:

(a) Calculate the standard costs of:
   (i)   a general health assessment;
   (ii) a medical assessment.   *(5 marks)*

(b) Prepare an operating statement for the period using detailed variance analysis to reconcile the standard cost of the new specialist unit with the actual cost of the new specialist unit.

(10 marks)

(c) Referring to your analysis in part *(b)*:
  (i) for each of the variances you have calculated, state one possible reason why it may have occurred; *(3 marks)*
  (ii) discuss the possible difficulties of using standard costing in this type of organisation.

(7 marks)

(Total = 25 marks)

© CIMA

25

Question from November 1998, CIMA

AZ Transport Group plc comprises three divisions – AZ Buses; AZ Taxis; and Maintenance.

AZ Buses operates a fleet of eight vehicles on four different routes in Ceetown. Each vehicle has a capacity of 30 passengers. There are two vehicles assigned to each route, and each vehicle completes five return journeys per day, for six days each week, for 52 weeks per year.

AZ Buses is considering its plans for the year ending 31 December 1999. Data in respect of each route is as follows:

| | Return travel distance (km) | | | |
	Route W 42	Route X 36	Route Y 44	Route Z 38
Average number of passengers				
Adults	15	10	25	20
Children	10	8	5	10
Return journey fares				
Adults	£3.00	£6.00	£4.50	£2.20
Children	£1.50	£3.00	£2.25	£1.10

The following cost estimates have been made:

Fuel and repairs per kilometre	£0.1875
Drivers' wages per vehicle per work-day	£120
Vehicle fixed cost per annum	£2000
General fixed cost per annum	£300 000

Required:

(a) Prepare a statement showing the planned contribution of each route and the total contribution and profit of the AZ Buses division for the year ending 31 December 1999.   (6 marks)

(b) (i) Calculate the effect on the contribution of route W of increasing the adult fare to £3.75 per return journey if this reduces the number of adult passengers using the route by 20%, and assuming that the ratio of adult to child passengers remains the same. (Assume no change in the child fare.)

   (ii) Recommend whether or not AZ Buses should amend the adult fare on route W.   (4 marks)

(c) The Maintenance division comprises two fitters who are each paid an annual salary of £15 808 and a transport supervisor who is paid an annual salary of £24 000.

The work of the Maintenance division is to repair and service the buses of the AZ Buses division and the taxis of the AZ Taxis division. In total there are eight buses and six taxis which need to be maintained. Each vehicle requires a routine servicing on a regular basis on completion of 4000 kilometres: every two months each vehicle is fully tested for safety. The Maintenance division is also responsible for carrying out any breakdown work, though the amount of regular servicing is only 10 per cent of the Maintenance division's work.

The annual distance travelled by the taxi fleet is 128 000 kilometres.

The projected material costs associated with each service and safety check are £100 and £75 respectively, and the directors of AZ Transport Group plc are concerned over the efficiency and cost of its own Maintenance division. The company invited its local garage to tender to the maintenance contract for its fleet and the quotation received was for £90 000 per annum including parts and labour.

If the maintenance contract is awarded to the local garage then the Maintenance division will be closed down, and the two fitters made redundant with a redundancy payment being made of 6 months' salary to each fitter. The transport supervisor will be retained at the same salary and will be redeployed elsewhere in the Group instead of recruiting a new employee at an annual salary cost of £20 000.

(i)   Calculate the cost of existing maintenance function.   (6 marks)

(ii) Advise the directors of AZ Transport Group plc whether to award the maintenance contract to the local garage on financial grounds.   (4 marks)

(iii) State clearly the other factors which need to be considered before making such a decision, commenting on any other solutions which you consider appropriate.   (5 marks)

(Total marks = 25)

© CIMA

26

Question 2 – May 2001, CIMA IDEC

VI plc produces a number of mobile telephone products. It is an established company with a good reputation that has been built on well-engineered, reliable and good-quality products. It is currently developing a product called Computel and has spent £1.5 million on development so far. It now has to decide whether it should proceed further and launch the product in one year's time.

If VI plc decides to continue with the project, it will incur further development costs of £0.75 million straight away. Assets worth £3.5 million will be required immediately prior to the product launch, and working capital of £1.5 million would be required. VI plc expects that it could sell Computel for three years before the product becomes out of date.

It is estimated that the first 500 Computels produced and sold would cost an average of £675 each unit, for production, marketing and distribution costs. The fixed costs associated with the project are expected to amount to £2.4 million (cash out flow) for each year the product is in production.

Because of the cost estimates, the Chief Executive expected the selling price to be in the region of £950. However, the Marketing Director is against this pricing strategy; he says that this price is far too high for this type of product and that he could sell only 6,000 units in each year at this price. He suggests a different strategy: setting a price of £425, at which price he expects sales to be 15,000 units each year.

VI plc has found from past experience that a 70% experience curve applies to production, marketing and distribution costs. The company's cost of capital is 7% a year.

Required:

(a) The Chief Executive has asked you to help sort out the pricing dilemma. Prepare calculations that demonstrate:
– which of the two suggestions is the better pricing strategy;
– the financial viability of the better strategy.   *(15 marks)*

(b) Discuss other issues that VI plc should consider in relation to the two pricing strategies.
(5 marks)

(c) Calculate and comment on the sensitivity of the financially better pricing strategy to changes in the selling price.   *(4 marks)*

(d) Discuss the usefulness of the experience curve in gaining market share. Illustrate your answer with specific instances/examples.   *(6 marks)*

(Total = 30 marks)

© CIMA

Question 2 – November 2001, CIMA IDEC

S & P Products plc purchases a range of good-quality gift and household products from around the world; it then sells these products through "mail order" or retail outlets. The company receives "mail orders" by post, telephone and Internet. Retail outlets are either department stores or S & P Products plc's own small shops. The company started to set up its own shops after a recession in the early 1990s and regards them as the flagship of its business; sales revenue has gradually built up over the last 10 years. There are now 50 department stores and 10 shops.

The company has made good profits over the last few years but recently trading has been difficult. As a consequence, the management team has decided that a fundamental reappraisal of the business is now necessary if the company is to continue trading.

Meanwhile the budgeting process for the coming year is proceeding. S & P Products plc uses an activity-based costing (ABC) system and the following estimated cost information for the coming year is available:

Retail outlet costs:

Activity	Cost driver	Rate per cost driver	Number each year for	
			department store	*own shop*
Telephone queries and requests to S&P	Calls	15	40	350
Sales visits to shops and stores by S&P sales staff	Visits	250	2	4
Shop orders	Orders	20	25	150
Packaging	Deliveries	100	28	150
Delivery to shops	Deliveries	150	28	150

Staffing, rental and service costs for each of S & P Products plc's own shops cost on average £300,000 a year.

Mail order costs:

Activity	Cost driver	Rate per cost driver		
		Post	*Telephone*	*Internet*
Processing "mail orders"	Orders	5	6	3
Dealing with "mail order" queries	Orders	4	4	1
Packaging and deliveries for "mail orders" – cost per package £10	Packages	2	2	1

The total number of orders through the whole "mail order" business for the coming year is expected to be 80,000. The maintenance of the Internet link is estimated to cost £80,000 for the coming year.

The following additional information for the coming year has been prepared:

	Department store	Own shop	Post	Telephone	Internet
Sales revenue per outlet	£50,000	£1,000,000			
Sales revenue per order			£150	£300	£100
Gross margin: mark-up on purchase cost	30%	40%	40%	40%	40%
Number of outlets	50	10			
Percentage of "mail orders"			30%	60%	10%

Expected Head Office and warehousing costs for the coming year:

Warehouse	2,750,000
IT	550,000
Administration	750,000
Personnel	300,000
	4,350,000

Required:

(a) (i) Prepare calculations that will show the expected profitability of the different types of sales outlet for the coming year. *(13 marks)*

(ii) Comment briefly on the results of the figures you have prepared. *(3 marks)*

(b) In relation to the company's fundamental reappraisal of its business,

(i) discuss how helpful the information you have prepared in *(a)* is for this purpose and how it might be revised or expanded so that it is of more assistance; *(7 marks)*

(ii) advise what other information is needed in order to make a more informed judgement. *(7 marks)*

(Total = 30 marks)

© CIMA

Question 3 – May 2001, CIMA IDEC

Division A, which is part of the ACF Group, manufactures only one type of product, a Bit, which it sells to external customers and also to division C, another member of the group. ACF Group's policy is that divisions have the freedom to set transfer prices and choose their suppliers.

The ACF Group uses residual income (RI) to assess divisional performance and each year it sets each division a target RI. The group's cost of capital is 12% a year.

Division A
Budgeted information for the coming year is:

Maximum capacity	150,000 Bits
External sales	110,000 Bits
External selling price	£35 per Bit
Variable cost	£22 per Bit
Fixed costs	£1,080,000
Capital employed	£3,200,000
Target residual income	£180,000

Division C
Division C has found two other companies willing to supply Bits:

X could supply at £28 per Bit, but only for annual orders in excess of 50,000 Bits.
Z could supply at £33 per Bit for any quantity ordered.

Required:

[Note: Ignore tax for parts *(a)* and *(b).]*

(a) Division C provisionally requests a quotation for 60,000 Bits from division A for the coming year.
   (i) Calculate the transfer price per Bit that division A should quote in order to meet its residual income target. *(6 marks)*
   (ii) Calculate the two prices division A would have to quote to division C, if it became group policy to quote transfer prices based on opportunity costs. *(2 marks)*

(b) Evaluate and discuss the impact of the group's current and proposed policies on the profits of divisions A and C, and on group profit. Illustrate your answer with calculations. *(11 marks)*

(c) Assume that divisions A and C are based in different countries and consequently pay taxes at different rates: division A at 55% and division C at 25%. Division A has now quoted a transfer price of £30 per Bit for 60,000 Bits.

Calculate whether it is better for the group if division C purchases 60,000 Bits from division A or from supplier X.

(6 marks)

(Total = 25 marks)

© CIMA

Question 3 – November 2001, CIMA IDEC

A & B manufactures cleansing products, which are sold either to retail stores for onward sale to the general public, or in bulk to cleansing companies in the food and hospital sectors.

The budgeted and actual information for the month just ended is:

Budget	Units	Selling price	Cost
Original Zest Cleanse	1,000,000	£0.40	£0.29
Lemon Zest Cleanse	1,200,000	£0.44	£0.30
Orange Zest Cleanse	800,000	£0.46	£0.31
Gloves	240,000	£3.00	£2.00
Canteen Clean (Food)	50,000	£30.00	£22.00
Hospital Anti-Bac (Hospital)	72,000	£35.00	£26.00

	Actual Units	Selling price
Original Zest Cleanse	950,000	£0.39
Lemon Zest Cleanse	1,360,000	£0.43
Orange Zest Cleanse	880,000	£0.47
Gloves	287,500	£3.00
Canteen Clean (Food)	46,000	£30.80
Hospital Anti-Bac (Hospital)	69,000	£35.10

When the company set the budget, the budgeted quantities were based on a forecast of the total market for each business sector, which was commissioned from a team of market consultants. This forecast proved to be inaccurate, as is shown in the table below.

Market data	Forecast units	Actual units
Cleanse products	8,000,000	8,500,000
Gloves	3,000,000	3,190,000
Food	400,000	360,000
Hospital	450,000	500,000

Information on retail products

Orange Zest Cleanse is a recent introduction and is a variation on, and an addition to, the company's range of Zest Cleanse retail products. Management is pleased with its sales so far. Savamart, the chief supermarket group, has recently repositioned the Zest Cleanse products on its shelves so that Lemon and Orange Zest are now at eye level and are situated above the Original Zest Cleanse.

A & B has entered into an agreement with another company to purchase a large number of household protective gloves. A & B is currently running a promotion based on these gloves. They are offered to retail customers who collect and send in tokens from the range of Zest Cleanse products together with a cheque for £3.

Information on bulk cleansing products

Over recent years, the market for Canteen Clean has decreased as factory canteens have reduced in number. This product is not suitable for small restaurants, which tend to use retail products or speciality stainless steel cleaners.

The market for Hospital Anti-Bac has grown steadily over the years. The introduction of private hospitals has caused the market to expand and as a result more companies have entered the market for cleansing products.

Required:

(a) Calculate the following variances in appropriate detail:
- sales margin price variances;
- appropriate sales margin mix variances;
- market size and market share variances for the different business sectors.

Summarise your calculations in a profit reconciliation statement. Assume that actual costs for each unit were the same as budget. *(18 marks)*

(b) Discuss the position revealed in each market sector and suggest areas where further investigation is needed. *(7 marks)*

(Total = 25 marks)

© CIMA

Question 4 – May 2001, CIMA IDEC

LM Hospital is a private hospital, whose management is considering the adoption of an activity-based costing (ABC) system for the year 2001/02. The main reason for its introduction would be to provide more accurate information for pricing purposes. With the adoption of new medical technology, the amount of time that some patients stay in hospital has decreased considerably, and the management feels that the current pricing strategy may no longer reflect the different costs incurred.

Prices are currently calculated by determining the direct costs for the particular type of operation and adding a mark-up of 135%. With the proposed ABC system, the management expects to use a mark-up for pricing purposes of 15% on cost. This percentage will be based on all costs except facility sustaining costs. It has been decided that the hospital support activities should be grouped into three categories – admissions & record keeping, caring for patients, and facility sustaining.

The hospital has four operating theatres that are used for 9 hours a day for 300 days a year. It is expected that 7,200 operations will be performed during the coming year. The hospital has 15 consultant surgeons engaged in operating theatre work and consultancy. It is estimated that each consultant surgeon will work at the hospital for 2,000 hours in 2001/02.

The expected costs for 2001/02 are:

	£
Nursing services and administration	9,936,000
Linen and laundry	920,000
Kitchen and food costs (3 meals a day)	2,256,000
Consultant surgeons' fees	5,250,000
Insurance of buildings and general equipment	60,000
Depreciation of buildings and general equipment	520,000
Operating theatre	4,050,000
Pre-operation costs	1,260,000
Medical supplies – used in the hospital wards	1,100,000
Pathology laboratory (where blood tests etc are carried out)	920,000
Updating patient records	590,000
Patient/bed scheduling	100,000
Invoicing and collections	160,000
Housekeeping activities, including ward maintenance, window cleaning etc	760,000

Other information for 2001/02:

Nursing hours	480,000
Number of pathology laboratory tests	8,000
Patient days	44,000
Number of patients	9,600

Information relating to specific operations for 2001/02:

	ENT (Ear, nose and throat)	Cataract
Time of stay in hospital	4 days	1 day
Operation time	2 hours	0.5 hour
Consultant surgeon's time (which includes time in the operating theatre)	3 hours	0.85 hour

Required:

(a) Before making the final decision on the costing/pricing system, management has selected two types of operation for review: an ear, nose and throat (ENT) operation and a cataract operation.

   (i) Calculate the prices that would be charged under each method for the two types of operation. (Your answer should include an explanation and calculations of the cost drivers you have used.)

(10 marks)

   (ii) Comment on the results of your calculations and the implications for the proposed pricing policy.

(5 marks)

(b) Critically assess the method you have used to calculate the ABC prices by selecting two items/categories above which you feel should have been dealt with in a different way. *(5 marks)*

(c) Explain whether the concept of throughput accounting could be used in a hospital.   *(5 marks)*

(Total = 25 marks)

© CIMA

31

Question 5 – May 2001, CIMA IDEC

JLX plc is a well-established manufacturing organisation that has recently expanded rapidly, by a series of acquisitions, in a period of favourable trading conditions. The need to integrate the management information and control systems of the rapidly expanding group has imposed a very large workload on the managerial and accounting teams. Consequently, some of the normal procedures at JLX plc have been neglected.

JLX plc uses return on investment (ROI) as the chief performance measure for controlling the operating activities of its divisions, and managers' bonuses are based on the achievement of ROI targets. The company also uses net present value (NPV) to assess and select investment projects. It used to be standard practice to assess and review all projects after implementation by a post-completion appraisal (PCA). However, PCA has been one area that has been neglected because of the increased workloads, and recently PCA has been applied only to those projects which have been considered unsuccessful.

PRO35 is a major project recently implemented by division X. This project was controversial because of its large capital requirement and high risk level. The Group Finance Director has stated that his department is now considerably under-staffed and that he requires more resources to operate effectively. In particular, he is using the need to carry out a PCA on PRO35 as a lever to gain more funds. He has told the Group Chief Executive that he thinks that PRO35 should be subjected to a PCA as he considers that it should be generating a greater return, given the continuing favourable trading conditions.

The Group Chief Executive has responded to this by saying that he feels that a PCA for PRO35 is unnecessary as it is generating the predicted net cash flow. To back this up, he cites the fact that division X's performance as measured by ROI is in line with its target. The Group Chief Executive has also said on several occasions that he is worried about behavioural issues if divisions are criticised and monitored unnecessarily.

Required:

[Note: Your answer must relate to the scenario above.]

(a) Evaluate whether it is advisable for an organisation such as JLX plc to carry out PCAs.

(7 marks)

(b) Discuss whether a PCA should be carried out on PRO35, a project that appears to be performing satisfactorily.

(5 marks)

(c) Critically evaluate the use of ROI as the performance measure within the JLX plc group.

(13 marks)

(Total = 25 marks)

© CIMA

Question 6 – November 2001, CIMA IDEC

(a) "Costing systems attempt to explain how products consume resources but do not indicate the joint benefits of having multiple products."

Required:

Explain the statement above and discuss:
(i) how the addition of a new product to the product range may affect the "cost" of existing products;
(ii) the consequences, in terms of total profitability, of decisions to increase/decrease the product range.

(10 marks)

(b) Telmat is a company that manufactures mobile phones. This market is extremely volatile and competitive and achieving adequate product profitability is extremely important. Telmat is a mature company that has been producing electronic equipment for many years and has all the costing systems in place that one would expect in such a company. These include a comprehensive overhead absorption system, annual budgets and monthly variance reports and the balanced scorecard for performance measurement.

The company is considering introducing:
(i) target costing; and
(ii) life cycle costing systems.

Required:

Discuss the advantages (or otherwise) that this specific company is likely to gain from these two systems.

(15 marks)

(Total = 25 marks)

© CIMA

33

Question 2 – May 2001, CIMA IMPM

PR plc is a marketing consultancy company that offers three different types of service. It is preparing the budget for the year ending 31 December 2002. The details for each type of service are as follows:

	Service A	Service B	Service C
Estimated demand (number of services)	150	800	200
	£ per service	£ per service	£ per service
Fee income	2,500	2,000	3,200
Consultant (£300 per day)	900	750	1,500
Specialists' report	400	200	500
Variable overhead	200	160	300

It has been estimated that the consultants will be able to work for a total of 2,400 days during the year. PR plc estimates that the fixed overhead for the year will be £600,000.

Required:

(a) *(i)* Prepare calculations that show how many of each type of service should be undertaken in order for PR plc to maximise its profits.

(ii) Prepare a statement that shows the budgeted profit for the year 2002 based on your answer to *(i)* above. *(8 marks)*

(b) The Managing Director has received the service schedule and budget statement that you prepared but would like it to be amended to reflect the following additional information:

There is a 90% learning curve operating on the consultants' times for service C. The budgeted consultants' time of 5 days per service C was based on the time taken for the very first service C performed. By the end of December 2001, a total of 100 type C services will have been performed.

The consultants' salaries will rise by 8% with effect from 1 January 2002.

Overhead costs will rise by 5% with effect from 1 January 2002.

Required:

Calculate the revised optimal service plan and prepare the associated profit statement for the year ending 31 December 2002. *(12 marks)*

(c) Prepare a report to the Managing Director that explains the implications of the learning curve effect on service C for PR plc. *(10 marks)*

(Total = 30 marks)

Note: The formula for a 90% learning curve is $y = ax^{-0.1520}$

© CIMA

Management & Cost Accounting: Professional Exam Questions. © Pearson Education Limited 2005

34

Question from May 1995, CIMA

A pharmaceuticals company has recently developed a new drug called Kabo, which is made using a continuous microbiological process. The process manager is responsible for material procurement.

Four material ingredients (K, A, B and O) are used in the processing of Kabo, all of which are obtainable from a variety of sources. The standard material requirements of 1 kg of Kabo are as follows:

k	0.33 kg	@ £104.00 per kg	£34.32
A	0.28 kg	@ £49.00 per kg	£13.72
B	0.23 kg	@ £186.00 per kg	£42.78
O	0.42 kg	@ £72.50 per kg	£30.45
Total	1.26 kg		£121.27

Process losses occur at an even rate throughout the processing operation and tend to rise if impurities are present in the ingredients. The effectiveness of Kabo depends on the quality of the ingredients being used and the maintenance of the ingredient mixture within close limits of that specified above.

At the start of April 1995, 318.6 kg of 40% processed Kabo were held in the division. At the end of April 426.3 kg of 52% processed Kabo were held. During April 831.0 kg of fully processed Kabo were transferred from the division to the stores. During April the following materials were acquired and input to the process:

K	291.6 kg at a cost of £30 006
A	242.6 kg at a cost of £12 421
B	198.2 kg at a cost of £37 262
O	392.0 kg at a cost of £26 719

Required:

As management accountant to the pharmaceuticals company,
1   In regard to the material input in April 1995, calculate:
   • the materials total cost variance
   • the materials price variance
   • the materials usage variance
   • the materials mixture variance, and
   • the materials yield variance.

Present these variances in the form of a financial control report for presentation to the company's management. You may assume that the opening and closing work-in-progress are subject to normal process losses only.   (16 marks)

2   Critically comment upon the following statement made by the company's finance director in regard to your report: *'This is an excellent report which tells us all we need to know for both*

financial and quality control purposes. We should pay the divisional manager a monthly performance bonus based on the cost variances that are reported.' (9 marks)

(Total marks = 25)

© CIMA

35

Question from Summer 1996, ICAI

Engineering Products plc manufactures a product PQR which is assembled from one component of P, one component of Q and one component of R.

The company is working to its full machining capacity of 30 000 hours per period but has sufficient assembly capacity to increase sales as and when required.

The PQR product is made in batches of 100. Data relating to machining hours and costs per batch of 100 components are as follows:

Component	Machine-hours	Variable costs (£)	Fixed costs (£)	Total costs (£)
P	25 hours	75	50	125
Q	50 hours	125	100	225
R	75 hours	150	150	300

The data relating to the variable and fixed costs of assembling a batch of 100 PQR products are as follows:

	£
Variable costs	300
Fixed costs	100

The selling price of one unit of PQR is £12.

The Marketing Director believes he could sell a minimum of 25% more PQR products in the period and probably up to 50% more, if there were additional machining capacity to cope with the additional production.

The Production Director has sourced a supplier who could manufacture each of the components and has agreed the following prices in batches of 100 manufactured components:

Component	£
P	150
Q	265
R	330

The Managing Director wishes to purchase only one type of component from the outside supplier (i.e. P or Q or R) which would then be assembled by Engineering Products plc.

Note: *Candidates can assume that there is no increase in total fixed costs in the Machining or Assembly Departments arising from increases in production.*

Required:

(a) Recommend which component should be purchased and how many should be purchased from the outside supplier, if 25% more products are to be produced and sold. (6 marks)

(b) Recommend which component should be purchased and how many should be purchased from the outside supplier, if the company is to produce and sell the maximum number of products up to a possible 50% increase. (6 marks)

(c) Contrast the profit earned in the period if no components are purchased from the outside supplier with the maximum possible profit which could be earned if one of the three components is purchased from the outside supplier. (8 marks)

(Total marks = 20)

© ICAI

36

Question 5 – November 2001, CIMA IMPM

ML plc was formed three years ago to develop e-commerce systems and design web sites for clients. The company has expanded rapidly since then and now has a multi-site operation with bases in the UK and overseas.

ML plc has recognised the need to formalise its planning and budgeting procedures and one of its divisional managers has been assigned to co-ordinate the budgets for the year to 31 March 2003. He recently attended a course on Financial Planning and Budgeting and has been puzzled by some of the concepts. In particular, he would like you to explain the following:

> The differences and similarities between zero-based budgeting and activity-based budgeting;
>
> The reasons why budget holders should prepare their own budgets;
>
> The reasons why incremental budgeting may not be appropriate as a basis of budgeting if budget bias is to be minimised.

Required:

(a) Prepare a report, addressed to the divisional manager, that explains the issues he has identified above.   *(15 marks)*

Techniques that are used in order to improve an organisation's performance include:

cost reduction; and

value analysis.

Required:

(b) Explain these techniques and how they may be used by ML plc as part of its planning activities.
(10 marks)

(Total = 25 marks)

© CIMA

Question 6 – November 2001, CIMA IMPM

SW Limited is a member of the SWAL group of companies. SW Limited manufactures cleaning liquid using chemicals that it buys from a number of different suppliers. In the past, SW Limited has used a periodic review stock control system with maximum, minimum and re-order levels to control the purchase of the chemicals and the economic order quantity model to minimise its costs.

The Managing Director of SW Limited is thinking about changing to the use of a just-in-time (JIT) system.

Required:

(a) As Management Accountant, prepare a report to the Managing Director that explains how a JIT system differs from that presently being used and the extent to which its introduction would require a review of SW Limited's quality control procedures. *(15 marks)*

SW Limited supplies its cleaning liquid to AL Limited, another company in the SWAL group, as well as selling to its external market.

SW Limited has capacity to produce up to 500,000 litres of cleaning liquid per week. The external market demand is 350,000 litres per week, and previously AL Limited demanded 100,000 litres per week. AL Limited has now advised SW Limited that it will require 250,000 litres per week from January 2002.

SWAL group policy:

1. evaluates the performance of group companies on the basis of their individual profits;

2. is to set transfer prices that will encourage the maximisation of group profits.

Required:

(b) Prepare a report to the group Management Team outlining how an appropriate transfer pricing policy would provide a satisfactory basis for appraising the performance of individual companies. Comment on the implications of this policy for the maximisation of group profits.
(10 marks)

(Total = 25 marks)

© CIMA

38

Question 3 – May 2001, CIMA IMPM

Exe plc is a motor car manufacturer. Exe plc has been in business for many years, and it has recently invested heavily in automated processes. It continues to use a total costing system for pricing, based on recovering overheads by a labour hour absorption rate.

Exe plc is currently experiencing difficulties in maintaining its market share. It is therefore considering various options to improve the quality of its motor cars, and the quality of its service to its customers. It is also investigating its present pricing policy, which is based on the costs attributed to each motor car.

Required:

(a) Discuss the significance to Exe plc of developing and maintaining communication links with suppliers and customers. *(15 marks)*

(b) Explain the benefits (or otherwise) that an activity based costing system would give Exe plc. *(10 marks)*

(Total = 25 marks)

© CIMA

39

Question 4 – May 2001, CIMA IMPM

(a) The WYE hotel group operates a chain of 50 hotels. The size of each hotel varies, as do the services that each hotel provides. However, all of the hotels operated by the group provide a restaurant, swimming pool, lounge bar, guest laundry service, and accommodation. Some of the hotels also provide guest entertainment, travel bureaux, and shopping facilities. The Managing Director of the group is concerned about the high level of running costs being incurred by the hotels.

Required:

Explain how cost reduction, value analysis and zero based budgeting techniques could be used by the WYE hotel group to improve the profitability of its hotels. *(15 marks)*

(b) M plc is a food manufacturer. It operates a just-in-time (JIT) system with computer-controlled, automated processing and packaging equipment. The focus of M plc's weekly management reports is on the variance analysis that is generated from a standard absorption costing system that uses labour hours as the basis of overhead absorption.

Required:

Explain why standard costing systems based upon absorption costing principles may be inappropriate in the modern manufacturing environment of companies such as M plc.
(10 marks)

(Total = 25 marks)

© CIMA

40

Question 5 – May 2001, CIMA IMPM

T plc, a food manufacturer, has determined the following standard cost details for the three ingredients that are blended together in the processing of one of its products:

Standard cost data for 1kg of product X:

0.5 kg of ingredient J @ £0.50 per kg	0.25
0.3 kg of ingredient K @ £1.20 per kg	0.36
0.25 kg of ingredient L @ £0.80 per kg	0.2
	0.81

Actual data for March 2001 was as follows:

Output of product X (000s kgs) 1,650

Raw materials used:

	Ingredient J	Ingredient K	Ingredient L
Quantity (000s kgs)	1,072	412	396
Cost (£000)	510	520	310

T plc does not hold any stocks of ingredients; instead, it acquires them on a just-in-time basis. It is now agreed that the standard price of ingredient J was unrealistic because of a worldwide shortage. A more realistic target would have been £0.55 per kg.

Required:

(a) For ingredient J, calculate the planning price variance and the operating price variance.

(4 marks)

(b) Explain why it is useful to analyse variances between planning and operating variances.

(4 marks)

(c) Calculate the individual material mix variances and the total material yield variance for March 2001.

(6 marks)

(d) Comment on the usefulness to management of individual material mix variances and the yield variance.

(4 marks)

(e) The deviations, in weight, from the standardised mix for the quantity input expressed as a percentage of the standardised weight for each ingredient are shown below:

Input: % deviation from standardised mix:

Management & Cost Accounting: Professional Exam Questions. © Pearson Education Limited 2005

60

	January	February
Ingredient J mix	10.4% (A)	14.1% (A)
Ingredient K mix	14.0% (F)	20.9% (F)
Ingredient L mix	4.2% (F)	3.2% (F)

These percentages are based on the following data:

	January 000 kgs	February 000 kgs
Output	1,000	1,800
Ingredient J	600	1,125
Ingredient K	280	468
Ingredient L	260	477

Required:

Calculate the corresponding values for March 2001 and comment on the usefulness of this type of analysis for operational control.   *(7 marks)*

(Total = 25 marks)

© CIMA

Answers

17

Question from Autumn 1995, ICAI

1

LAVENDER LIMITED – OPERATING STATEMENT FOR SIX MONTHS ENDED 30 JUNE 1995

Note 1:
From the presentation of the information in the question, it is clear that marginal costing is being used, i.e. fixed production overhead is not absorbed into products, nor is fixed selling overhead absorbed into cost of sales, however variable selling costs are absorbed into cost of goods sold. Thus, expenditure variances can only be calculated for fixed production overhead and fixed selling overhead. Had an underlying absorption costing system been used, the fixed production overhead would have been absorbed into units produced and fixed selling costs would also have been absorbed into cost of units sold. Therefore, there would be an output level volume variance and a fixed selling cost volume as well.

	Actual results (000s) 900	Flexible-budget variance	Flexible budget (000s) 900	Sales-volume variance	Static budget (000s) 1,000
Activity level (sales)		£		£	£
Sales revenues (£11 per unit)	9,650		9,900		11,000
Variable costs					
Direct materials	4,300		4,500		5,000
Direct labour	1,700		1,800		2,000
Variable production overhead	905		900		1,000
Variable sales overhead	975		855		950
Total variable costs (£8.95)	7,880		8,055		8,950
Contribution margin (£2.05)	1,770		1,845		2,050
Fixed costs					
Fixed production overhead	1,350		1,305		1,350
Fixed selling overhead	265		200		200
Total fixed costs	1,570		1,550		1,550
Operating income	200		295		500

Reading off the summary variances:

Flexible budget variances:

Sales price	250,000 A
Total direct material	200,000 F
Total direct labour	100,000 F
Total variable overhead	5,000 A
Total variable selling overhead	120,000 A
= Contribution margin flexible budget variance	75,000 A
+ Total fixed production and selling overhead variance (expenditure only)	20,000 A
= Flexible budget variance of operating income	95,000 A
+ Sales margin volume variance	205,000 A
= Static budget variance of operating income	300,000 A

2   The total flexible budget variances can be analysed into price and efficiency effects:

a   **Price variances**

(Budgeted price × Actual quantity produced or sold) – Actual total cost

Note 2:

Actual quantity **produced** will be used to calculate the production cost variances, while actual quantity **sold** will be used to calculate the selling cost variances (both fixed and variable). The fixed production costs are not absorbed into the product unit, so no production-volume variance can be calculated for them. The fixed production and fixed selling costs are not absorbed into units to be sold, so no volume variances arise for them.

	£
Sales price variance:	
(900,000 × 11.00) – £9,650,000	= 250,000

Note: using (11.00 – 10.722222) × 900,000 will involve candidates in using the non-truncated decimal version of the difference between unit budgeted and actual selling price, and some rounding in order to get the right answer. Students who use this approach should check it against the variance calculated on the total basis. This comment also applies to the other variances below.

	£
Variable selling cost expenditure variance (0.95 × 900,000) – £975,000	= 120,000 A
Fixed selling cost expenditure variance (200,000 – £265,000)	= 65,000 A
Direct material price variance (5 × 900,000) – £4,300,000	= 200,000 F
Direct labour rate variance (2 × 900,000) – £1,700,000	= 100,000 F
Variable production overhead expenditure variance (recovery rate is based on budgeted direct labour hours) (5.0 × 180,000) – £905,000	= 5,000 A
Fixed production overhead expenditure or budget variance (£1,350,000 – £1,305,000)	= 45,000 F
Total price variances	**95,000 A**

b   Efficiency variances

Budgeted price × (Actual quantity used – Budgeted quantity allowed to make the actual output)

Note 3:
No sales efficiency variance can be calculated for sales revenue or for sales cost variances.

Direct material efficiency	Nil
Direct labour efficiency	Nil
Variable overhead efficiency	Nil

See below – Note 4

Total flexible budget variance   £95,000 A

Note 4:
No standard costing information has been given, such as the standard allowance per unit of output, which could allow the efficiency variance to be calculated. However, it can be obtained by deducting the price/expenditure/rate variances from the total flexible budget variances.

	Total flexible budget variances	–	Price/rate/expenditure variances
DM	£200,000 F		£200,000 F
DL	£100,000 F		£100,000 F
Var. Prodn. O/head	£5,000 A		£5,000 A

Therefore, all the efficiency variances are nil.

Sales margin volume variance captures the impact on profit of the sales volume being different from budgeted levels. As the units sold are valued at marginal cost, and fixed selling overhead is not absorbed into units sold, this is measured completely in terms of budgeted unit contribution margin:

[Budgeted quantity sold – Actual quantity sold] × £2.05	=	$(1,000,000 – 900,000) \times £2.05$
	=	$100,000 \times £2.05$
	=	£205,000 A

3 COMMENTS ON THE REVISED OPERATING STATEMENT

To: Production Director

From: Management Accountant

Re: Comments on the Revised Operating Statement

The insertion of the Flexible Budget between actual and static clearly shows the sales margin volume variance of £95,000 A and the flexible-budget variance of operating income of £205,000 A. The fact that there was a shortfall of 100,000 units sold compared to budget meant that there was a shortfall in profit, based on the sales performance.

On the cost side, the flexible budget variances are much greater and show that the main reason for the shortfall in the actual profits against budget is the cost performance. These flexible budget variances give a proper insight into the cost performance as there is no volume effect clouding the comparison of actual against budget; the flexible budget being flexed to the actual level of sales activity achieved.

Thus it is necessary to explore the flexible budget variances more closely and identify those which are material in amount.

Sales margin price		£250,000 A
Direct materials price	£200,000 F	
Direct labour rate	£100,000 F	
Variable production overhead expenditure		£ 5,000 A
Variable sales overhead expenditure		£120,000 A
Fixed production overhead expenditure	£ 45,000 F	
Fixed selling overhead expenditure		£ 65,000 A
Total variances analysed	£345,000 F	£440,000 A
Total flexible budget variance of operating income		£95,000 A

As can be seen from the above analysis, the production cost variances all show favourable variances, but the sales performance largely contributed to the poor actual profit; sales price was less than budget by £0.28 pence, which had a negative impact on actual profit, to the extent of £250,000 A. Variable and fixed selling costs were also high-spending areas and yet actual sales volume dropped below budget, by 100,000 units. Thus, the spending on variable and fixed selling costs needs to be pruned and subjected to a value for money audit.

22

Question 2 – November 2001, CIMA FMAF

(a)

Workings

Budgeted profit
Labour   (3 mins ÷ 60 mins) × £10 =   £0.50
Material   £0.75
Variable overhead   (35% of labour) =   £0.175
Fixed overhead   (40% of labour) =   £0.20
Standard profit per unit   £0.375

Therefore, budgeted profit = 59,500 units × £0.375/unit = **£22,312.50**

Total sales margin variance
2,500 units × £0.375/unit = **£937.50 F**

Material cost variance
No variance as actual and standard costs are both £0.75/unit.

Labour wage variance
Actual rate = £38,500 ÷ 3,500 hrs = £11/hr
Variance = (£10/hr – £11/hr) × 3,500 hrs = **£3,500 U**

Labour efficiency variance
Standard hours = (3 mins ÷ 60 mins) × 62,000 units = 3,100 hrs
Variance = (3,100 hrs – 3,500 hrs) × £10/hr = **£4,000 U**

Variable overhead expenditure variance
Standard expenditure = 35% of direct labour (£10/hr) × 3,500 hrs = £12,250
Variance = £12,250 – £9,500 = **£2,750 F**

Variable overhead efficiency variance
Variance = (standard hours – actual hours) × standard variable overhead rate =
(3,100 hrs – 3,500 hrs) × £3.50/hr = **£1,400 U**

Fixed overhead expenditure variance
Budgeted expenditure = £0.20/unit × 59,500 units = £11,900
Variance = £11,900 – £9,500 = **£2,400 F**

Fixed overhead volume variance
Variance = (budgeted volume – actual volume) × standard fixed overhead rate = (59,500 units – 62,000 units) × £0.20/unit = **£500 F**

Actual profit

		£	£
Sales	(62,000 units × £2/unit)		124,000
Labour		38,500	
Materials	(62,000 units × £0.75/unit)	46,500	
Variable overheads		9,500	
Fixed overheads		9,500	
			104,000
			20,000

Operating statement reconciling budgeted and actual profit

	£	£
Budgeted profit		22,312.50
Total sales margin variance		937.50 F
Labour wage variance	3,500 U	
Labour efficiency variance	4,000 U	
Variable overhead expenditure variance	2,750 F	
Variable overhead efficiency variance	1,400 U	
Fixed overhead expenditure variance	2,400 F	
Fixed overhead volume variance	500 F	
		3,250.00 U
Actual profit		20,000.00

(b)

Possible reasons for labour efficiency and labour wage variance:

Labour efficiency variance: unfavourable
Staff may have been poorly trained and may be inexperienced. Also, the benefits structure within the firm may not sufficiently motivate staff, thereby causing inefficiency.

Labour wage variance: unfavourable
Better educated and hence higher-paid labour may have been employed. Also, a higher wage may have been introduced to enhance incentives for workers.

(c)

The calculation of the overhead absorption rate should attempt to reflect as accurately as possible the source of the overheads in the cost centre. This should, however, be weighed against the costs of trying to devise an accurate absorption rate.

SS Ltd calculates the overhead absorption rate using direct labour costs as its base. This is acceptable as SS Ltd has a single wage rate across the entire company. The overhead rate would thus be the same if the absorption rate were based on labour hours. Note also that the firm only produces one product, so the overheads per unit will be the same regardless of the system used to calculate the absorption rate.

23

Question 3 – November 2001, CIMA FMAF

(a)

Cash budget

	January	February	March	Total
Sales	1,500	16,500	47,500	65,500
Cash invested	15,000	0	0	0
Total cash inflow	151,500	16,500	47,500	65,500
Salaries	22,500	22,500	22,500	67,500
Capital expenditure	25,000	37,500	37,500	100,000
Serviced offices	19,500	6,500	6,500	32,500
Variable production costs	1,200	4,200	8,000	13,400
Marketing and advertising	10,000	0	5,000	15,000
Administration overhead	300	500	500	1,300
Total outflow	78,500	71,200	80,000	229,700
Net cashflow	73,000	(54,700)	(32,500)	(14,200)
Add: balance from previous month	0	73,000	18,300	0
Cash balance at end of month	73,000	18,300	(14,200)	(14,200)

Workings:

Sales receipts
Total sales are to be £200,000. The breakdown per month is:
January: 15% of £200,000 = £30,000
February: 30% of £200,000 = £60,000
March: 55% of £200,000 = £110,000

Sales receipts

	January	February	March	Total
5% deposit	1,500	3,000	5,500	10,000
45% paid a month later	0	13,500	27,000	40,500
50% paid two months later	0	0	15,000	15,000
Sales receipts	1,500	16,500	47,500	65,500

Salaries
(6 employees × £45,000 per annum) ÷ 12 months = £22,500 per month.

Capital expenditure
The total cost of capital is £100,000. 25%, or £25,000, of this is to be paid as deposit in January. 37.5%, or £37,500, is to be paid in both February and March.

Adminstration overhead

	January	February	March	Total
60% in month used	300	300	300	900
40% paid a month later	0	200	200	400
Total paid	300	500	500	1,300

(b)

It is apparent that the cashflow position of T Ltd gets worse month on month. Under these circumstances, lending institutions are very unlikely to lend the company any money, fearing that it will be unable to make interest payments. T Ltd, therefore, has to devise ways to improve the first quarter cashflow situation. This could be done in several ways.

Clients could be asked to pay a larger deposit on contracts. This may, however, drive business to competitors and worsen cashflow, rather than improve it.

Staff numbers could be cut with due consideration for the viability of the business under a smaller workforce.

Marketing and advertising costs are arguably a luxury at this stage, and such expensive campaigns could be implemented later under better cashflow conditions.

A larger investment could be requested from the venture capitalist.

(c)

There are several advantages of using a spreadsheet in the preparation of the cash budget. For example, spreadsheets significantly reduce the time needed for the budgeting process. A general proforma has to be entered into the program, and only the figures have to be entered thereafter, with the program doing most of the calculations. This would also allow T Ltd to quickly assess other budgeted scenarios. The budget can easily be modified to incorporate new figures, and can be used to make comparisons with actual figures.

26

Question 2 – May 2001, CIMA IDEC

(a)

The mathematical relationship underlying the cumulative average-time learning model is $y = pX^q$, where

y = cumulative average time per unit
X = cumulative number of units produced
p = time required to produce the first unit
q = rate of learning

Now,

$q = \ln 0.7 \div \ln 2 = -0.51457$

Therefore, the cost of the first unit is:

$p = 675 \div (500^{-0.51457}) = £16,523.90$

Average cost per unit with 15,000 units is:

$y = 16,523.90 \times 15,000^{-0.51457} = £117.28$

Average cost per unit with 6,000 units is:

$y = 16,523.90 \times 6,000^{-0.51457} = £187.93$

Evaluation of the better pricing strategy: (i) 15,000 units @ £425 each or (ii) 6,000 units @ £950 each:

Strategy 1

Units	Cost per unit	Total cost	Incremental cost
15,000	117.279	1,759,189	0
30,000	82.096	2,462,870	703,681
45,000	66.636	2,998,620	535,750

		Year 1	Year 2	Year 3
Sales revenue	(15,000 × £425)	6,375,000	6,375,000	6,375,000
Learning curve cost		−1,759,189	−703,681	−535,750
Cash flow		4,615,811	5,671,319	5,839,250

Strategy 2

Units	Cost per unit	Total cost	Incremental cost
6,000	187.927	1,127,562	0
12,000	131.549	1,578,588	451,026
18,000	106.777	1,921,986	343,398

		Year 1	Year 2	Year 3
Sales revenue	(6,000 × £950)	5,700,000	5,700,000	5,700,000
Learning curve cost		−1,127,562	−1,578,588	−1,921,986
Cash flow		4,572,438	5,248,974	5,356,602

It is evident, therefore, that selling 15,000 units at £425 each is the better pricing strategy given the greater cash inflow.

Financial viability of Strategy 1:

	Year 1	Year 2	Year 3
Cashflow	4,615,811	5,671,319	5,839,250
Fixed costs	−2,400,000	−2,400,000	−2,400,000
Net cashflow	2,215,811	3,271,319	3,439,250

Year	Total cashflows	Discount rate	NPV
0	−0.75	1.000	−0.750
1	−5.00	0.936	−4.675
2	2.216	0.873	1.935
3	3.271	0.816	2.669
4	4.939	0.763	3.768
			2.947

Workings
Year 0 cashflow: £0.75 million in immediate development costs
Year 1 cashflow: £3.5 million in assets + £1.5 million in working capital
Years 2 and 3 cashflow as per the table above
Year 4 cashflow: £3.439 million + £1.5 million in replacement of obsolete working capital

All in all, it is apparent that Strategy 1 is a viable option, as the NPV is positive over the project's total duration of 4 years.

(b)

Other issues that VI plc should consider in relation to pricing strategies are:

VI plc may place greater emphasis on gaining market share, and may therefore want to lower the price below £475 to achieve this aim.

VI plc may face stiff competition, so careful evaluation of competitors' prices needs to be made. Also, demand levels for VI plc's products need to be assessed.

VI plc may not want to price its product too low for fear of portraying a low-costs, low-quality image.

(c)

VI expects demand to be constant, and at a volume of 15,000 units a year, expects a constant stream of revenue of £6,375,000 each year (in years 2, 3 and 4). In NPV terms this means £15,631,500. At the point of indifference, the present value of sales must be £15,631,500 − £2,947,000 = £12,684,500. So, the per unit price could be £12,684,500 ÷ 15,000 units = £345 per unit.

The project seems not to be sensitive to the selling price, but a competitor could force prices down below £345 if it can exploit better learning curve cost advantages.

(d)

The learning curve can effectively ensure that a company gains a large market share within a given time period. However, learning curves cannot be generated without some form of previous experience in the product being sold.

All things being equal, a firm stands to gain a larger slice of the market, the lower is the price of its product. It is, therefore, helpful if a firm can set a price lower than initial cost to achieve this. However, a price war could ensue if companies attempt to out-price each other in this fashion.

Practical examples of the above can be seen quite frequently. This is particularly true of Far Eastern firms entering Western markets in high-tech goods, steel, the automotive industry, etc. The consequences have not only been lower prices across the board, but often political opposition to such entry in the form of tariff barriers and quota restrictions.

30

Question 4 – May 2001, CIMA IDEC

(a)

(i)

Direct costs

Theatre cost per hour	£4,050,000 ÷ (300 × 4 × 9) =	£375
Pre-operation cost per operation	£1,260,000 ÷ 7,200 =	£175
Consultants' fees per hour	£5,250,000 ÷ (2,000 hrs × 15) =	£175

Indirect costs – patient care

Nursing	£9,936,000
Linen and laundry	£920,000
Kitchen and food	£2,256,000
Medical supplies	£1,100,000
Pathology laboratory	£920,000
Total	**£15,132,000**

Indirect costs – admissions

Updating records	£590,000
Patient/bed scheduling	£100,000
Invoicing	£160,000
Total	**£850,000**

Indirect costs – facility

Housekeeping	£760,000
Insurance	£60,000
Depreciation	£520,000
Total	**£1,134,000**

Patient care cost per day = £15,132,000 ÷ 44,000 patient days = **£343.91 per day**
Admission cost per day = £850,000 ÷ 9,600 patients = **£88.54 per patient**

Indirect costs have been split into three groups so as to get a better handle on what is the driver of each cost. Patient days have been selected as the driver for patient care costs, as these costs increase with the length of the patients' stay. Patient numbers is the driver for admissions costs, as these are likely to increase or decrease with the number of patients admitted. Facility costs have not been allocated a cost driver, as the mark-up is to cover these costs.

We can now work out prices under the existing system and under ABC for both the ENT and the cataract operations.

For an ENT operation:

Existing system		*ABC system*	
Direct costs	£	Direct costs	£
Operation £375 × 2 hrs	750.00	Operation £375 × 2 hrs	750.00
Pre-operation costs	175.00	Pre-operation costs	175.00
Consultant's fee £175 × 3 hrs	525.00	Consultant's fee £175 × 3 hrs	525.00
	1,450.00		1,450.00
Mark-up of 135%	1,957.50	Patient care £343.91 × 4 days	1,375.64
Price	**3,407.50**	Admission	88.54
			2,914.18
		Mark-up of 15%	437.13
		Price	**3,351.31**

For a cataract operation:

Existing system		*ABC system*	
Direct costs	£	Direct costs	£
Operation £375 × 0.5 hrs	187.50	Operation £375 × 0.5 hrs	187.50
Pre-operation costs	175.00	Pre-operation costs	175.00
Consultant's fee £175 × 0.85 hrs	148.75	Consultant's fee £175 × 0.85 hrs	148.75
	511.25		511.25
Mark-up of 135%	690.19	Patient care £343.91 × 1 day	343.91
Price	**1,201.44**	Admission	88.54
			943.70
		Mark-up of 15%	141.56
		Price	**1,085.26**

(ii)

Under the ABC system, the proposed price for both the ENT and the cataract operations is lower than those under the existing pricing system. This being so, the mark-up may be increased in order to maintain the same aggregate level of profit as under the existing system.

It is apparent from the above calculations that there is a considerable drop in price using the ABC system for the cataract operation. The short-stay nature of the operation consumes fewer support resources, such as admissions procedures and patient care days. This type of operation is currently over-priced, and may be pushing patients to seek treatment elsewhere.

(b)

The two items chosen for special consideration are given below. Note that any other combination would be acceptable too.

Pathology laboratory costs
These costs have been lumped together with others, which are driven by the length of patients' stay. However, not all patients who stay for treatment require use of this facility. So the cost burden should fall on those patients who actually require this facility. An alternative cost driver for this cost could be the number of tests performed, i.e. £920,000 ÷ 8,000 tests = £115 per test. This would allow a more accurate pricing plan per patient.

Nursing costs

It is apparent that nursing costs are significant in relation to the total costs. Therefore, they should be broken down as far as possible so as to allow a more detailed examination of what is driving these costs. The breakdown should take into consideration the type of work completed, the skills required to do this, the pay per hour of doing a particular task, etc. The fact that the figure for nursing hours is so high suggests that 'nursing' entails a range of activities, which can eventually be broken down further.

(c)

Throughput accounting can be used in this context, with the bottleneck being bed occupied, operating theatre, intensive care bed, or specialist skill, etc. This would ensure that the hospital's scarce resources are used to maximum advantage.

Note, however, that throughput accounting is used primarily to speed up processes. This is not ideal in a hospital environment, where patients' health is at risk. Performance measures based on throughput alone would, therefore, be counter-productive. Other measures such as patient death, recovery times, etc, should be used as effective performance measures for a hospital too. Nonetheless, throughput may help in managing resources more efficiently.

32

Question 6 – November 2001, CIMA IDEC

(a)

(i)

The cost of some activities often depends on the number of production runs. For example, machine set-up or quality inspections fit into this category. The longer the production run, the fewer set-ups or inspections have to be carried out, as opposed to many short production runs. Similarly, there will be more set-ups and inspections if the company produces more than one product. Thus, the total cost of these activities increases. Nonetheless, there are benefits in having multiple products. The demand for certain products may be seasonal in nature (e.g. ice cream), so a second product may smooth out production and sales. Multiple products can also help a company increase revenue by building an image around its products.

(ii)

In deciding whether or not to expand the product range, all relevant costs need to be considered, not just production costs. It is easy to overlook cost reduction possibilities in other areas when a new product is added to the portfolio. Marketing costs, for example, can be reduced as a new product will benefit from the already established brand name. Furthermore, having a wide range of products can actually be necessary for profitability. Consider a stationery store that sells nothing but paper. It is unlikely that this store will be profitable if a competitor provides not only paper, but pens, pencils, diaries, etc. Customers will almost definitely switch to the supplier with the larger product range in this case.

(b)

Telmat is involved in a rapidly-changing business, as technology moves from voice-only communication to voice-and-text messaging systems. Both target and life-cycle costing could help Telmat in this unstable environment.

(i)

Target costing replaces traditional standard costing. This may be to Telmat's advantage because it puts pressure on managers to keep costs to a bare minimum. This has the added benefit that staff may learn to be more creative and innovative in trying to keep costs down. New, more efficient production processes may be developed, for example. Target costing is also more flexible than standard costing, as it takes time to develop standard costs. Targets can be amended as and when necessary, and this flexibility is crucial in a rapidly-changing industry. Above all, target costing considers the price that customers are willing to pay for a product. In this case, Telmat is thus forced to be more outward looking, and hence more competitive. Target costing involves participation from all levels of staff. Managers and workers need to communicate ideas frequently in order to achieve the targets.

(ii)

Given the nature of the industry, Telmat's products are likely to face a very short life cycle. The estimation of life-cycle costs helps the firm to establish whether a product will be able to generate profit quickly enough in the face of such a short product life. Most costs in the high-tech industry are likely to be incurred at the design stage, and life-cycle costing will help managers in their attempt to contain the high initial costs. Life-cycle costing also takes into consideration the time to launch a new product on the market. It is often necessary to launch new products timely in order to be profitable. Finally, life-cycle costing can help in avoiding unprofitable projects by assessing the likely costs over the entire life cycle.

36

Question 5 – November 2001, CIMA IMPM

(a)

Zero-Based Budgeting (ZBB) is a budgeting system which entails that all activities and their associated costs need to be justified. There are no rollover figures from previous budgeting periods, so managers have to justify all figures from scratch (or from 'zero').

Activity-Based Budgeting (ABB) is a budgeting system that focuses on the costs incurred by each activity, and the significance of each activity in relation to the performance of the business.

ZBB and ABB are similar in that managers are required to assess the activities with the company and determine whether they should take place. However, ABB distinguishes between value adding and non-value adding activities. It thus motivates managers to cut down on non-value adding activities.

Budgeting is an important process in management. It motivates managers in that they feel included in the organisation's decision-making process. They are thus likely to want to improve performance. It is also more likely that managers will achieve targets as they are working to a plan.

Incremental budgeting is a budgeting system that determines future budgets on the basis of adjustments to previous budgets, and is therefore quite the opposite of ZBB. In general, previous numbers are adjusted for volume and price changes. The justification for activities is not assessed.

Budgetary slack refers to the inclusion of additional costs in budgets, so that managers do not necessarily have to meet a rigidly set figure, but can operate within a range. Budgetary slack is more likely to occur in incremental budgeting than under ZBB or ABB.

(b)

Cost reduction refers to the permanent reduction of the cost of a unit of output without compromising quality. Value analysis refers to customer's perception of the value of a product.

ML plc develops e-commerce solutions for clients, and has operations in different countries. This suggests that activities are possibly duplicated in each country. It is important, therefore, to identify all activities and pinpoint duplication. The nature of e-commerce would suggest that duplication can be overcome by transferring products from one operation to another at different stages of the production cycle. Each operation would contribute to the development of the product in a different way.

Although it may seem sensible to have one UK-based operation completing the entire product in order to streamline the production process, a presence in different markets may be necessary. This presence affects clients' perception of the value of the product.

38

Question 3 – May 2001, CIMA IMPM

(a)
The value chain is the sequence of business functions in which utility is added to the product of an organisation. To thrive in the modern business environment, businesses need to consider all aspects of the chain in bringing to market high-quality products at low cost. The value chain considers the following business areas:

Suppliers
Research and development
Design of products
Production
Marketing
Distribution
Customer Service

The value chain emphasises that looking solely at refining the production process through automation, for example, is not enough. In Exe plc's case, the company would stand to gain by focusing also on suppliers and customers. A just-in-time system is most appropriate in this context.

By receiving all the necessary parts from suppliers as and when needed, Exe plc would cut down on stock-related costs. This would include warehousing and general wear and tear (if the parts are not further processed quickly enough). Similar logic applies on the customer side. Exe plc should produce cars as and when required by customers, rather than accumulate a large stock of cars to sell over, say, the next 5 years. Again, this cuts down on stock-related costs. Increased communication with suppliers and customers is of paramount importance in successfully operating a JIT system.

Exe plc could potentially improve its market share by cutting costs related to maintaining high levels of stock and thereby becoming more price-competitive.

(b)
Activity-based costing is a system that allows overhead costs to be allocated in more economically meaningful ways than traditional costing. In traditional costing, overheads are usually allocated to individual units of production via an absorption rate, such as machine hours. This is often unsuitable, as machine hours may not be driving the costs.

In contrast, ABC aims to identify the cause for a particular overhead, and allocates overheads on the basis of this cost driver. This allows managers to make a more informed judgement about the level of resources being consumed in producing a particular product. Pricing decisions will also be more accurate.

Exe plc stands to benefit from the implementation of an ABC system, especially in view of its present pricing policy. Each model of car will generally have consumed different levels of resources in production. Lumping all overheads together and attributing them to each car on a single basis (e.g. machine hours) is likely to under- or over-cost certain models, and thus under- or over-price them too (if a cost-plus approach to pricing is assumed). ABC refines the costing side, and thus leads to more accurate and meaningful pricing.

Question 4 – May 2001, CIMA IMPM

(a)

Cost reduction aims to reduce the unit cost of a service without compromising quality. WYE hotel group would do well to reassess its overheads, especially whether they are being allocated in an economically sensible way to each service and whether certain overheads need to be incurred at all.

Value analysis aims to examine all the factors that increase the value of the product in question. This would allow WYE to understand how to cut non-value adding costs, thereby increasing profitability.

Zero-based budgeting (ZBB) is a system of budgeting that requires managers to justify each activity. Past budget figures are not used as a guide to divisional requirements. Managers have to justify their costs from scratch. ZBB encourages managers to think about whether certain activities are at all necessary. This again encourages focusing on value-adding activities.

(b)

M plc operates a highly-automated production process. Absorption costing relies mainly on allocating overheads on a labour hour basis. It is unlikely that labour is the main cost driver for overheads in this case.

Standard costing and variance analysis compare actual costs to standard costs. In a JIT environment, the emphasis is on keeping stock levels low. Standard costing is based on large batch sizes and stock levels, however, in order to minimise unit cost.

In a modern production environment, most costs are not volume-related. Increasingly, costs are becoming more facility-related. Standard absorption costing focuses on unit costs, which is misleading. M plc should, therefore, look at other methods.

To be competitive in the modern business environment, companies need to focus on being innovative and improving existing processes. Standard costing encourages reliance on predetermined standards, which are difficult and expensive to review frequently. There is little motivation to exceed the standard once achieved.

of character; a strong concern for detail and a tendency to check everything personally to make sure that nothing has been overlooked.

Implementer (IMP): turns concepts and plans into working procedures; plenty of self-discipline, combined with realistic, practical common sense; a practical organiser, translating policy decisions into easily understood procedures, then getting on with the work. This person likes structure and order and dislikes mess and chaos. Because of an essentially practical orientation, many nursery nurses are naturally in the Implementer role.

Monitor Evaluator (ME): this team member is particularly good at analysing problems and evaluating ideas and suggestions with an objective mind and the ability to think critically; able to analyse huge quantities of data; this person is most likely to identify the flaws in an argument and to stop the team from committing itself to a misguided project.

Team Worker (TW): this is often the most sensitive member of the group, very aware of the needs and worries of the other team members and is able to sense undercurrents; a good communicator; a good listener; he or she promotes unity and harmony so that the team, as a whole, works better when the Team Worker is there – things are different if he or she is absent.

Plant (PL): this team member contributes by putting forward new ideas and strategies; the most imaginative and intelligent member of the team, most likely to come up with radical new approaches; the person who is likely to provide the solution to a problem.

Belbin concluded that good teams would be much easier to form in organisations if thought were given to the team-role composition of natural working groups.

It is worth investing time and effort also into a good induction programme, as it will meet important objectives, such as gaining greater employee loyalty, developing a stronger managerial base for future promotions or ending gender and racial inequalities. Later on, you may be expecting your new recruit to participate in recruiting and developing their own replacement as they move up the career ladder, so it is important to establish solid foundations.

Induction generally falls into two parts. The period between the appointment and taking up the post should be used for providing information on timetables, curriculum matters and other general information. A visit to the centre is useful for giving this information if it can be arranged. For the initial period in post, junior members of staff may be placed under the general guidance of a colleague whom they can call on for help with minor problems. This is known as *mentoring*.

Large nurseries or day care centres may have formal induction programmes covering the first weeks in the post. Alternatively, you may have to invent a programme for your new member of staff and this is best done *together* with that new member of staff.

In the nursery

With any new team member, it is important – on day one – to outline the expectations and limits of both the individual concerned and the existing team. One good way is to write down what you expect of the new employee and, perhaps more importantly, what your new recruit can (and is prepared to) offer. Go gently on formalising the relationship; some people may balk at the idea of having too many demands put upon them in the early stages. In any case, this 'agreement' will, obviously, change and be superseded as the new staff member settles into the job. Ideally, your relationship is going to be a long term one. Use an appropriate job description for this purpose. See Samples 42–47, pages 212–220.

GOOD PRACTICE

Try to put yourself into the new person's shoes and anticipate their needs. It is natural for the new recruit to suffer from a feeling of isolation at first in the new environment. This is where a mentor becomes invaluable.

A mentor is someone who can challenge, support, advise, motivate and encourage your new member of staff. It must be someone who understands the work and believes in the potential of the new recruit. A mentor will provide a safe harbour for the new team member – a space to ask questions, think out loud, make mistakes without feeling embarrassed or quashed. A good mentor will view the new recruit objectively and give constructive feedback along with general guidance.

In the nursery

The mentor could be you – the nursery manager – but it is generally more effective if it is a colleague who is more senior than the new recruit (but not intimidating) or who is at the same level but who has been in the job for long enough to know the ropes. If the mentor is also the manager of the recruit, the recruit will be so anxious to please that they may find it difficult to ask unguarded questions. Similarly, do not put a new recruit into the care of a mentor who is already a friend of the new recruit (for instance, knew them at college) as true friends are rarely objective enough about each other. Use Samples 58–60 (which can be adapted for your own purposes) as a system for mentoring the skills of the new staff member.

See Samples 58–60, pages 234–241.

Teams, team roles and team building

We commonly use the expression 'the whole is greater than the sum of the parts' without stopping to consider what it might mean. The importance of having an effective team in a child care context cannot be underestimated. Here we will explore management theory that will assist the manager in putting together a good whole – a good team.

The concept of 'team' can be quite elusive: it is evident that people may function as a team without being part of a working group. Conversely people may belong to the same working group without constituting a team. The essence of a team is that its members form a co-operative association through a division of labour that best reflects the contribution that each can make towards the common objective. The members do not need to be present at the same place and at the same time to enable the team to function.

THE CHARACTERISTICS OF A TEAM

It is helpful to explore the characteristics of a team. In any organisation a good team will:

- work together
- share a common aim
- co-operate with others
- share/communicate/support between it's members
- have motivation for the task in hand
- have catalytic relationships so that new ideas are extended
- be committed to the task and the team
- be comprised of members who each understand their own role in the team and are reliable in it
- complete the task.

Clearly if a team does not or will not fulfill these criteria then it will not be a good team and will not best serve the needs of the organisation. Management theorists have, therefore, spent time and effort working out how and why teams work.

TEAM ROLE MODELS

A theorist called Meredith Belbin spent many years observing teams at work and re-designing these teams to see if productivity improved. From this work he built a *team role model* (1981) which identifies how individuals are likely to work within a team and how to put together combinations of individuals to get the best results.

Most teams are commonly made up of members holding particular roles. They are there by virtue of the position or responsibilities they represent. No overall sense of design governs the composition of the group which, in human terms, is little more than a random collection of people with as wide a spread of human foibles and personality characteristics as one might expect to find in the population at large.

Nevertheless it is clear that the compatibility of members of the team is crucial to its effectiveness. The question of the interaction of members within a team become more important the more often a team meets. It is a subject of no less importan than whether members of a team are qualified to be Nursery Assistants or Office in-Charge. The problem is that human compatibility is more difficult to assess th technical competence. Belbin's experiments and fieldwork give some leads on h the subject of compatibility within teams might be approached.

Belbin's studies showed that there are eight 'team roles' that people will assu in a group, as listed below.

Resource Investigator (RI): the team member who explores and reports on idea developments outside the group; good at making external contacts and at conc ing negotiations; usually outgoing and relaxed, with a strong inquisitive sense; al ready to see the possibilities inherent in anything new.

Co-ordinator (Co): the person who controls the way the team moves forwards tov it's objectives by making the best use of the team's resources; good at recogn where the team's strengths and weaknesses lie; good at ensuring that the best made of the potential of each member of the team; sometimes acts as the cha son of the group but need not be the official leader of the team; this person tal ily, listens carefully and basically trusts people.

Shaper (SH): this person shapes the way in which the team effort is applied, dir attention to the setting of objectives and priorities and seeking to impose shape or pattern on group discussion and on the outcome of group activitie ious, dominant and extrovert, full of nervous energy, the shaper is outgoin tional, impulsive and impatient but has nervous energy and commitmen ensure that the team remains task-orientated and able to achieve.

Completer/finisher (CF): protects the team from mistakes of both commissi omission, actively searches for aspects of works which require a more tha degree of attention and maintains a sense of urgency within the team; ha of concern with order and purpose and usually has good self-control and

In practice there are a multitude of reasons why well-balanced teams are unlikely to form spontaneously. People are often picked for working groups because it is sensed that they have characteristics akin to those who are already there. So redundancies in some team-roles will be associated with shortages in others. At higher levels of responsibility similar team-role types are found because the organisation favours and rewards with promotion those with particular styles of approach.

One of the prime obstacles to many managers utilising a team-role approach is that an unchangeable staffing structure precludes entry into the team of the most suitable individuals. This raises the question of how a good team can be formed in a nursery which is not recruiting nor likely to transfer people from the jobs they currently hold. However, if there is any room for manoeuvre, there are potential benefits for managers of the team role model, as outlined below.

Recruitment

When a new staff member is being sought, what sort of person should the nursery look for? The orthodox, almost reflex response, is for a nursery to search for someone who fits the image of those who are already there. Fewer problems then arise in mutual adjustment between the newcomer and his or her established colleagues. However, in team-role terms the more fundamental need is for someone who will fill the team-role gap in the group. This cannot be ascertained without completing a team-role inventory of colleagues and examining what is missing. Once this is done a personal specification can be drawn up of the general shape of the candidate the nursery needs to recruit. The interview now becomes directed towards the key question that the selectors will be posing to themselves: how far does the candidate match the personal specification?

Internal reshuffling

The second immediate benefit of using team-role concepts relates to internal postings. Managers have reported advantages in being able to make bolder moves than they would otherwise contemplate through confidence that the appointee will contribute the team-role that is lacking. This occurs typically where the experience which the incoming staff member brings with her or him is not altogether appropriate but his or her natural orientation and behaviour more than compensates for any deficiency in technical knowledge. (The converse point is also important: internal postings that suggest themselves for technical reasons could be questioned once the implications of the move in team-role terms have been explored.)

Protecting viable partnerships

A common mistake is to underestimate the dynamic factors that bind together the smallest team of all. Pairings (such as Nursery Officer in Charge and her Deputy) of proven effectiveness are often broken up to fill managerial gaps (e.g. to cover maternity leave in another nursery) or even as well-intentioned acts of management development, with little realisation of how much the *interdependence* of these two people contributes to the running of a successful unit. (In industry, successful twosomes are more stable in top management than on the way up. A Chairman and a Managing Director who establish a good working relationship maintain it to the benefit of the enterprise as a whole. In contrast, any junior executive pair which does well will seldom be seen as anything other than two able individuals.)

TEAM BUILDING

Establishing the right climate in which well-designed teams can form and flourish is the foundation stone on which more effective teamwork in the future can be built. Only then does it become possible to explore the many questions raised by trying to create an optimum combination of people. The merits of each potential member can be raised in terms of what they technically can contribute and the roles they are likely to play in the group that is being formed. Once this process starts one finds that some people have more to contribute than others irrespective of what it is they have to offer. Designing a team engenders a search for individuals who are good examples of their type. Team-building is an art in that everyone is different and combinations of different people are not wholly predictable.

Once the team has been put together, the free exchange of opinions in that team – whether it be in industry or in the child care service – is vital for the success of that team. There are enormously pleasurable aspects of team work such as succeeding as a team and sharing praise. Where criticism and correction are necessary they need to be offset by praise and thanks. The people around you will blossom or wither depending on the balance between the encouragement and the criticism that you give to them.

For a manager, the ability to support and lead a group is critical not just to the well being of the staff concerned and for the organisation, but also to give you enormous support and strength.

GOOD PRACTICE

Team work is about *trust*, giving staff the opportunity to develop decision-making skills. Good team players give their staff the facts and let them have a say in decisions that affect them.

The following guidelines will help you to empower your staff.

Delegate, don't dump: delegating is an essential working practice but many managers do not understand what it actually means. If you give away only unpleasant tasks, that is dumping and your staff will consider it, correctly, as an abuse of power

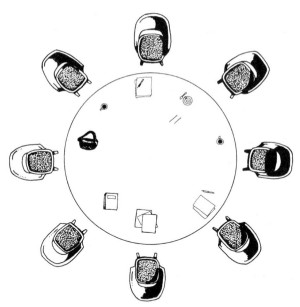

Set up for a productive team meeting

and trust. Delegation is giving something away that can help develop someone else's expertise, allowing enough authority to get it done.

Follow through: effective team members remember the promises they make, take the appropriate course of action and let their colleagues know what has been done. If you tell someone that you are going to check on something for them, do it. (If you do not intend to do something, never say you will. Your credibility will go down each time your staff's expectations are not met.) It is a good idea always to carry a notebook when you have a meeting. If you say you are going to do something, let others see that you are writing it down. This signifies that you mean business. Review your notebook regularly and give your staff updates on progress.

Set goals within the team: research has shown that regular goal setting improves performance more than any other team working technique. Define people's work in terms of goals and objectives that become a basic part of each job description, not something extra or tacked on. To be effective motivators, the goals must be clear and attainable. If possible, each goal should be stated in terms of what the team member must do rather than what the outcome should be. Write everything down.

Encourage everyone to have plans for their future: if your staff feel they cannot move up, they will move out. The possibilities of promotion or of fresh challenges are important motivators. When people feel they can grow in their jobs, they are more likely to work harder at them. Team members should be undergoing training to enable them to fill better positions in the future.

Minimise stress (see also Chapter 9) by ensuring that lines of communication all the way to the top are accessible to everyone, especially the most junior staff. You might have weekly discussions, where group members are able to identify their collective sources of stress. From there, team members can go on to isolate their problems and deal with them.

Give positive feedback to individual staff members in front of the others. A simple 'Thanks, you did a great job with Mrs Jones – she was very anxious' further boosts morale and makes the team user friendly.

KEYS TO GOOD PRACTICE

- Always look at any person you are about to appoint and ask yourself whether this person is a suitable role model for the children.
- With respect to promotions, all internal applicants should have the courtesy of a private discussion with their line manager whether they are short-listed or not.
- In the event of an internal short-listed candidate not being appointed, they should be given a feedback interview at the earliest possible opportunity.
- Make sure any new member of staff is introduced to the parents, and their photo and name put on the parents' board before they arrive. This applies at whatever level the appointment is made.
- Care must be taken when appointing staff to take references from former employees, and to arrange police and health checks.
- Some police departments charge for making police checks. Small nurseries find this outlay very onerous. It is quite in order to ask new members of staff to meet this cost in the first instance with the monies to be refunded after a specified period of time.
- When a new staff member joins the team, a mentor should be nominated to assist the settling in process.
- A regular appointment should be made with the new team member to check the induction process.
- It is important to recognise that any new member joining the team will alter the dynamics within the group. Give thought to the development of the team and to the place of any new member in the team.

---

8 HUMAN RESOURCING FOR QUALITY CHILD CARE

What this chapter covers:
- staffing and training
- National Vocational Qualifications (NVQs)
- appraisals
- self-appraisal

This chapter is about working with people, about career development and guidance and support for staff. It is about familiarity with the child care standards to which staff should be performing. It is about recognising where performance falls short of the standards and about taking steps to rectify the situation.

Staffing and training

In the labour-intensive business of child care, staff are key to the success of the enterprise. It is good management practice to ensure that staff feel valued and stimulated by their work and have opportunities for training and development. Staff will need to feel they have the ongoing support of the manager or management team, and will require a clear understanding of the aims of the unit (see also sections on *motivation* in Chapter 3). It is important that the staff feel they are part of a stable and consistent work team; continuity of staffing has obvious benefits for the children.

GOOD PRACTICE

This can be achieved by:
- establishing pay and conditions of employment which reflect the responsibility undertaken by the carers as well as their skill and abilities;
- having a clear staffing policy and selection procedure;
- allowing time for staff meetings and regular supervision;
- identifying staff training needs and finding training opportunities.

Throughout this text issues which lend themselves to in-house staff development have been identified.

PRE-SERVICE TRAINING

Pre-service training is offered to young and mature students in further education colleges and some training agencies. Details of this provision can be found by contacting your Local Education Authority or local library. In recent times the availability of education and training courses has not remain static for long so it is important to keep abreast of developments in pre-service training and managers must develop strategies for this purpose.

One good method of keeping abreast of developments in training provision is to offer the nursery as a training venue to the local college. This means you will have access to up-to-date information from the course you are servicing.

Having students in the nursery has cost implications because, while their enthusiasm and energy is a welcome addition to the staff group, their training needs must be taken seriously and guidance, instruction and supervision must be made available to them. However, having a training unit means that staff are aware of standards required at all times.

It is also important to communicate the role of students to the parents using the centre.

IN-SERVICE TRAINING

Both qualified and unqualified staff may now be offered National Vocational Qualifications (NVQs) if the nursery is part of or has access to an Assessment Centre. Help with this is available from the Awarding Body validating the NVQ. This body will also be able to assist you with titles of useful texts to help you structure the underpinning of knowledge for these candidates.

IN-HOUSE STAFF DEVELOPMENT

Training can take the form of 'on the job' opportunities supplemented by external courses, events and seminars. Budgets for training will, of course, need to be included at an early stage in the provision for running costs. To supplement this work and incorporate fresh experiences a list of training opportunities is available from the:
- local authority – both education and social services departments
- local college – this also covers topics such as administration and computer training
- National Children's Bureau – this agency publishes a list of vocational seminars each year.

TRAINING REQUIREMENTS

There are certain training components that are required by law. These are:
- 50% of staff must hold recognised qualifications to meet the needs of the Children Act
- at least one member of staff should hold a Food Handler's Certificate if food is served on the premises
- at least one member of staff should hold a current First Aid Certificate or equiv-

alent issued by the Red Cross or St John's Ambulance Brigade. This requirement should be checked with the local day care advisor as it varies from authority to authority.

It is also desirable to have staff specifically trained in the following areas:

- managing children's behaviour
- HIV awareness
- equal opportunities
- multicultural curriculum
- keeping children's records
- child protection.

In the nursery

In-service training is an essential part of the on-going work and development of the staff in child care. Providing good quality child care requires considerable skill and abilities. By offering training and learning opportunities, staff are helped to develop their full potential to the benefit of the child care service they are providing.

See Sample 50, page 224.

National Vocational Qualifications (NVQs)

NVQ awards were introduced for staff already involved in vocational work – be it full time or part time, waged or unwaged. There is a series of NVQs specifically designed for those working in child care and education.

A candidate may be assessed for an NVQ without having gained any previous qualifications or undertaken any previous courses or forms of study. However, they will have to show that they have the required underpinning knowledge and understanding of child care in order to be assessed for the award.

There are no examinations – NVQ candidates are assessed on their performance in the work setting against a set of national standards. Assessment is carried out by qualified assessors from the candidate's workplace or by peripetetic assessors who operate from the local NVQ Assessment Centre.

There are four NVQs in Child Care and Education at Level 2. This level of NVQ is designed for those staff who work under the supervision of others. There are five NVQs at Level 3, designed for staff who work without supervision or in supervising others. Each of the qualifications is a combination of core units and endorsement units. Core units represent work carried out in a wide range of child care settings. Endorsement units represent more specialised areas of work.

To achieve an NVQ at either level, a candidate must be assessed as competent in all of the core units and in all of the units in one endorsement. The choice of endorsement must reflect the candidate's work setting, e.g. those in day care would undertake 'Group Care and Education', while class room assistants would undertake 'Working in Support of Others'.

NVQs are relevant to the manager and can be used in achieving the following objectives in the workplace:

- as a means of staff development, for both qualified and unqualified staff
- as a means of quality upgrading, by focusing on the National Occupational Standard Working With Young Children and their Families (NOSWWYCF)
- as a method of supervision, by assessing the work of colleagues
- as a means of self development, by becoming an Assessor or Verifier.

THE NVQ AS A MEANS OF DEVELOPMENT AND QUALITY UPGRADING

NVQs may be used as a helpful framework for developing staff at all levels and for improving the quality of the service.

Unqualified staff

Staff who, for various reasons, are not qualified but work well with the children will be able to gain recognition for their existing skills and be assessed for additional skills by undertaking the NVQ in 'Child Care and Education'. They can start work in the areas where they feel confident and, by careful planning and support, move into the more difficult units. This allows supervision of these candidates.

Staff development for qualified staff

Qualified staff can add to their academic achievements by undertaking an Advance Diploma in Childcare and Education or other programmes which are offered in further and higher education establishments.

Qualified staff can be encouraged to train as Assessors for NVQ. The training as such is not difficult and staff grow enormously from the process (although assembling documentary evidence to prove their competence can be daunting – the Awarding Bodies are working towards helping staff with this issue).

Assessors are trained under the Employment Occupational Standards Council who publish and control the assessment standards. They are the industry lead body for training and development, employment and personnel.

The assessor award can be made specifically for child care by CACHE (CACHE insist that the child care assessors they register hold *occupational competence*), or as a non-specific award by other bodies. The assessor award has excellent development potential and has been the catalyst for much progression since NVQs were first offered in child care in 1990/91.

A further development at the NVQ Level IV is Management of Care which has supervisory management units taken from the Management Charter Initiative as well as other vocationally selected areas.

The assessing of both sorts of training has the effect of improving the quality of child care because familiarity with the National Occupational Standard Working With Young Children and their Families (NOSWWYCF) means that staff are constantly confronted with the details of good practice.

A copy of NOSWWYCF should be available whether or not the nursery is involved with NVQs.

The process of supervising staff can be combined with the assessing role and the trust which will develop around the advice and counselling can only enhance the cohesion and confidence of the team.

Appraisals

Appraisals are regular meetings between manager and subordinate, providing a non-threatening routine occasion when work standards can be discussed and suggestions for improvement can be jointly decided upon.

Conducting an appraisal

Appraisals can either be bottom-up or top-down:
- bottom-up – that is from parents to nursery officers, from nursery officers to managers, from managers to day care supervisors, until Director of Social Services is arrived at. This system is very popular and widely used in America but has never really taken hold in the UK.
- top-down – from Director of Social Services, heads of functional units to heads of sections to managers and so to nursery staff. This is the system most commonly used in this country.

Appraisals are designed to assess and improve performance and to suggest training input where appropriate. In some systems, again generally in American companies, performance scores are kept although these are probably not appropriate for the child care service.

THE PURPOSE OF A PERFORMANCE APPRAISAL SYSTEM

There are a number of possible reasons for introducing performance appraisal in a child care service organisation. These include:
- providing feedback on individual staff performance
- providing staff with a basis for self evaluation
- providing a non-threatening routine occasion when work standards are discussed
- establishing and monitoring objectives and targets
- reviewing salary, conditions of service and other rewards
- providing a basis for promotion, dismissal, probation etc.
- diagnosing training and career development needs
- maintaining equity in treatment of staff
- discovering individual (and nursery) potential
- monitoring the effectiveness of policies and procedures.

Experience of the appraisal process within a large number of organisations suggests that not all these purposes can be achieved within one appraisal scheme, and that any institution has therefore to make careful selection of the key purpose that it wishes the scheme to serve.

In practice it is possible to classify three general types of scheme:
- those that are related to personnel management needs, e.g. upgrading discipline
- those that are primarily concerned with improving current and future performance in the child care service, e.g. curriculum, children's review
- those that are designed to develop the individual and the team, e.g. to uncover training needs.

In the nursery
All appraisal documentation, such as prompt sheets and forms, needs to be considered carefully. Examples are provided in Appendix A. It will be necessary to adapt these materials to make them suitable for use in a particular nursery. This work might be carried out by the whole staff or by a representative staff working group depending on the size of the nursery. In addition to ensuring documentation is suitable for use in a particular nursery, steps should be taken to produce appraisal forms which are consistent with other nursery documents.

See Samples 51–57, pages 225–233.

OPEN VERSUS CLOSED QUESTIONS

When conducting an appraisal interview with a member of staff, consider what type of questions to ask to gather the information required, e.g. open questions, closed questions, probing questions, reflective questions, and so forth.

Although closed questions are useful for checking specific pieces of information, open questions will usually allow for long informative answers. Even open questions need to be chosen carefully. Questions that begin with 'why?' may reveal less than those that begin with 'how?' or 'what?'. The first tends to suggest that a justification is required, the others ask for an explanation or description of a process.

For example: avoid *'Do you think those children are badly behaved?'* (closed)

'How's the curriculum planning group – no difficulty?' (closed)

Ask   *'What do you think of those children?'* (open)

'Tell me about your plans for the curriculum.' (open)

Always try to avoid questions which suggest that one answer is expected rather than another.

Appraisal interviews

BEFORE THE APPRAISAL INTERVIEW

- Issue self-appraisal forms to staff and arrange the time and place well in advance.
- Decide what information you want to collect from the interview. Make a list of important points to be covered.
- Aim to be systematic; plan to collect all the information about one area before moving on to another. Try to bear in mind a picture of the complete interview in terms of the information to be collected, rather than in terms of the questions to be asked.

AT THE START OF THE INTERVIEW

- Clearly explain the purpose of the interview and agree an agenda for the meeting that is acceptable to both parties.
- Make the staff member to be appraised feel comfortable and able to talk freely. Remember that an effective appraisal is a two-way discussion, and you need to address the issues raised by the staff member.

DURING THE INTERVIEW

- Focus on the responsibilities and goals of the appraisee rather than on their character traits.
- Make notes, as you will not remember enough detail to do so afterwards, particularly if you are conducting a number of appraisal interviews; however, avoid making notes in an officious way.
- Do not try to do things in the interview which are best done at another time and in a different way, e.g. give out work for the following week or discuss a key child.
- Where appropriate, explore the answers that the staff member gives you. Do not assume that because he or she has talked after you asked a question, the information you wanted was given.
- Deal constructively with disagreement; if both of you are discussing the important issues in performance there will often be a legitimate difference of view

about what should be done. A good appraisal is an opportunity for tackling such disagreements in a constructive way.

- Deal constructively with apathy. If the staff member appear apathetic about the process (e.g. 'What's the point?') deal with the issue of apathy; if you do not, the interview will be a waste of time. You may have to arrange another appointment.
- Do not be aggressive or ask trick questions.
- Avoid showing excessive approval, disapproval, scepticism or even surprise.
- Ask one question at a time. Multiple questions are confusing for everyone (especially avoid multiple questions which confuse information with judgements: e.g. 'What outings have you arranged for your group, or don't you get on well with their parents?').
- Once you have asked a question, wait for an answer; short silences are not necessarily a bad thing and may get a nervous person talking.
- Let the colleague finish what he or she is saying without interruption.
- Listen carefully (see the Activity on page 105) and concentrate on what the staff member is saying; do not talk unnecessarily yourself.

AFTER THE INTERVIEW

- Ensure that agreements made in the appraisal are acted upon and that agreed deadlines are met.

BENEFITS OF APPRAISAL

The benefits of appraisal are:
- performance improvement
- identification of training needs
- facilitation of decision making
- monitoring the health of the organisation
- increased motivation and productivity.

Appraisal will assist the manager to:
- increase staff performance
- improve motivation and commitment
- keep staff well informed
- have more insight and better relationships
- reduce the likelihood of unforeseen difficulties.

Activity
Study the above list of benefits of introducing an appraisal system. Are there any more that you can think of? Make your own list.

DIFFICULTIES OF APPRAISAL

Listed on page 123 are some of the main problems nurseries have encountered when implementing appraisal systems for the first time.

- Employees fear unfair or subjective judgements and therefore find the process threatening.
- If the appraisal is badly conducted, it is very demotivating.
- Management reluctance to tackle performance problems and conduct reviews often has to be overcome.
- Inadequate training in the concept and processes, often the result of undue haste, causes systems to fail.
- Failure to see performance review management as a continuing process limits the benefits.
- Unnecessary elaboration limits user appeal.
- Lack of top management commitment to the process, as well as the idea, limits credibility.
- Trying to introduce systems that are alien to the culture raises the risk of rejection.
- Trying to introduce systems faster than the existing culture can absorb them results in patchy implementation.
- Failure to communicate the new values prevents acceptance of benefits.

Activity

Study the above list of difficulties of introducing an appraisal system. Are there any more that you can think of? Make your own list.

In the nursery

It is essential that staff are made familiar with the aims of the appraisal system and with the procedures. The documents should be taken to the staff meeting and discussed fully before any attempt is made to put the system in place.

See Samples 51–60, pages 225–241.

Self-appraisal

Self-appraisal has come to be seen both as an important ingredient in any formal appraisal scheme and as valuable for any nursery worker or teacher. Within an appraisal scheme, self-appraisal can occur at a number of points.

- Self-appraisal may be a useful form of preparation for an appraisee before an initial meeting. At this point, self-appraisal can help to clarify possible areas to put forward for development during the rest of the appraisal process.
- Self-appraisal can also be useful immediately before the appraisal interview. Placed at this point in the process, it can help the appraisee to come to the interview prepared and with his or her own thoughts in order.
- Self-appraisal can also be encouraged by the way in which the different components of the appraisal process are arranged. For example, child observation, targeted towards agreed areas and followed by feedback and discussion will encourage self-appraisal.

Self-appraisal can therefore contribute successfully at several points during the appraisal process.

Within a formal appraisal scheme, self-appraisal can be approached in various ways, as follows:

- putting aside some time for quiet, unstructured reflection
- free writing, i.e. writing about your job and how you feel it is going in an unstructured way
- writing about your job with reference to a job description or list of key tasks
- writing about your job and how you feel it is going, with the help of a few prompting questions
- using a self-rating prompt sheet, where you are asked to rate your performance in various aspects of your work according to a numerical or verbal scale (see Sample 56, page 231)
- listing various tasks, for which you are responsible, and ranking them in order of the success you feel you have achieved in them
- completing prompting sentences which help you to explore the various aspects of your work
- evaluating your performance in the light of previously agreed objectives and criteria of success.

In essence, all these approaches are designed to facilitate personal reflection. The best approach is a matter of individual taste through the different approaches do tend to vary in their emphasis.

Self-appraisal should not only be seen as part of the appraisal process. It is also, in a more or less informal way, a regular feature of nursery work. It is a rare child care worker who does not reflect upon how an activity went or on what came out of a meeting. Indeed, one aim of a formal appraisal scheme might well be to encourage this form of on-going reflection, perhaps making it more targeted and constructive. However, whether self-appraisal is formal or informal, certain difficulties can occur.

Look out for the following problems in carrying out self-appraisal.

- *The 'blindspot'*: people can be unaware of a particular strength or weakness or may simply prefer to ignore them. Structured appraisal prompt lists may help staff to focus on all aspects of their job, and make it more difficult to overlook particular areas.
- *Being too self-critical*: some people, especially those with an internal locus of control, are excessively hard on themselves, minimising successes and agonising over difficulties. In these cases, self-appraisal could become an exercise in self-criticism and prove an unsettling experience.
- *Confidentiality*: the question arises as to whether comments recorded during self-appraisal should be shared directly with the appraiser.

CASE STUDY

These difficulties are outweighed by the many benefits of self-appraisal, as the following nursery workers tell us:
'The whole process wouldn't have been much good without it (self-appraisal).'

'I think that development has to come from self-analysis. Once you recognise what you need to do, you're more likely to go ahead and do it.'

In the nursery

Self-appraisal can:
- bring about individual commitment to change
- ensure that appraisal is a two-way process
- ensure that the appraisee clarifies his or her thoughts before meeting the appraiser and thus knows what he or she wants from the process
- bring about a greater feeling of professionalism, for at the heart of professionalism is the concept of self-monitoring
- encourage the habit of on-going reflection, carried out in a constructive spirit and on the basis of a desire to celebrate success and to work on improvements.

See Samples 54–60, pages 229–241.

KEYS TO GOOD PRACTICE

- On-going staff development is an essential part of nursery life. Ensure a regular development programme is in place. Include (1) in-house items for all staff (e.g. curriculum, procedures) and (2) external input (e.g. from colleges, local authority, NCB, Open University, Open College).
- A copy of NOSWWYCF should be available in the nursery, whether the centre is involved in NVQs or not.
- Staff appraisal should be adopted as an invaluable technique for quality supervision.
- Self-appraisal should be viewed as a valuable tool for a child care worker.

9 STRATEGIES FOR MANAGING CHANGE IN QUALITY CHILD CARE

> **What this chapter covers:**
> - management of change in the child care service
> - management of stress in staff
> - management of stress in self

This chapter is about the only sure thing in life, apart from death and taxes. It is about change. Just to survive, even in the most sanguine profession, change has to be lived with, even relished, as part of the dynamic nature of society.

It is particularly difficult for front line workers in child care to cope with the changes in their own organisations and in the lives of parents when the children they are caring for so desperately need stability and routine.

This chapter looks at the various facets of change and suggests ways of dealing with them. This will include stress, at an organisational level and staff level, and particularly at the manager's level.

Management of change in the child care service

In recent years the child care service, like all other services, has experienced an accelerated pace of change.

Charles Handy in his book *The Age of Unreason* uses a frog metaphor: 'if you put a frog in water and slowly heat it, the frog will eventually let itself be boiled to death. We too, will not survive if we do not respond to the radical way in which the world is changing.'

It is part of the manager's role to identify those changes which will affect the work of the team and those which will not, or at least not yet. The manager should:
- identify changes which could affect the centre's work
- assess the urgency of such changes
- develop strategies to implement the changes
- resettle the team's procedures after the changes have been implemented.

Managers who are proactive, as opposed to reactive, will suffer less personal pain (stress) as a result of change. Charles Handy tells us that 'to suffer less disturbances from the unexpected we must understand the past'.

In response to this atmosphere of change Tom Peters produced his text *Thriving on Chaos* in which he extols us to enjoy and welcome change and to 'roll with the ambiguities'.

Other organisational theorists suggest similar tactics, for the truth is there is no choice.

The child care worker must become two tactically different workers – one with the children, conserving routines, reverencing systems and creating stability, and the other with the organisation, introducing computers, accepting new forms of training with students, changing their shift systems, changing their expenditure patterns and, in some cases, even changing their employers.

Change in the child care service brings inherent conflict and it is important for managers to be clear about this and not to make the mistake of thinking that the only way to sanity is to rush down the path of change. The children, their routines and the pattern of their lives, as far as the centre is concerned should remain stable on a daily basis. Transitions, in the best interests of the children, should be gradual.

Changes which could affect the service are:

- changes in law, both children's and employment law
- changes in the curriculum demanded by parents and others
- changes in the health of the population locally or nationally
- changes in training programmes for child care workers
- changes in economics affecting parents, salaries and funding systems.

On the occasion of any one of these events, the manager will be expected to lead the team to a new way of working.

A good example of multiple changes to the service was the 1989 Children Act. The implementation of this Act was particularly stressful, coinciding as it did with other related changes, namely:

- school management reform – the option for schools to opt out of local authority management
- training reform – the introduction of NVQs for child care and education workers
- curriculum reform – the introduction into schools of the National Curriculum
- standards reformed (or asserted) by the publication of the National Occupational Standards for Working With Young Children and their Families
- acknowledgement of the world recession and the affect on small businesses
- public awareness of HIV
- the ratification of the UN convention on children's rights
- the appearance of the corporate nurseries.

In London the situation was further complicated by the birth pangs of the newly identified education departments hastily set up following the demise of the ILEA in 1991.

Thus the child care world was inundated with change.

Strategies to deal with such changes need to be developed.

A MNEMONIC FOR MANAGING CHANGE

C Communication systems and consultation systems must work effectively in the nursery

R Responsibilities and duties of all staff must be understood

E Effects must be monitored (using the evaluation system described in Chapter 4)

A Aims and purposes of change – and the possible effects on the children – must be known and understood

M Morale must be maintained (in the team and consequently in the nursery)

As you can see, the strategies listed are very much the strategies we have been examining and which constitute good management practice with a heavy emphasis on communication. The following section suggests some strategies which will assist in developing non-threatening communications systems.

Activity

The aim of this activity is to learn to distinguish between rewarding and punishing behaviours.

Review the following lists and add any other punishing or rewarding behaviours that come to your mind. Think about your own inter-personal style and see how many of these specific behaviours you can identify in your day-to-day patterns of working with others. These behaviours also apply in your private life, of course, as well as in work situations. Ask yourself the very blunt questions: 'To what extent do people voluntarily seek me out; to what extent do they take the initiative in contacting me, communicating with me, sharing ideas and viewpoints with me, and including me in their personal and social activities?'

The answers to these questions will give you the clearest possible indication of whether your management style is primarily that of a punisher or a rewarder. In the long-term, a rewarding style of dealing with others tends to keep your own stress level to a minimum, it helps others to do the same; and it makes work life a pleasant, enjoyable, achievement-oriented process.

Rewarding behaviour	Punishing behaviour
Talking positively and constructively	Making others feel guilty
Affirming the feelings and needs of others	Soliciting approval from others excessively
Treating others as equals whenever possible	Losing one's temper frequently or easily
Stating one's needs and desires honestly	Playing 'games' with people; manipulating or competing in subtle ways
Delaying automatic reactions; not flying off the handle easily	Throwing 'gotchas' at others; embarrassing or belittling others
Levelling with others; sharing information and opinions openly and honestly	Telling lies; evading honest questions; refusing to level with others
Confronting others constructively on difficult issues	Overusing 'should' language; pushing others with words
Staying on the conversational topic	Displaying frustration frequently
	Making aggressive demands of others

until others have been heard	Diverting conversation capriciously; breaking others' train of thought
Stating agreement with others when possible	Disagreeing routinely
Questioning others openly and honestly; asking straightforward, non-loaded questions	Restating others' ideas for them
	Asking loaded or accusing questions
	Overusing 'why' questions
Keeping the confidences of others	Breaking confidences; failing to keep important promises
Giving one's word sparingly and keeping it	Flattering others insincerely
Joking constructively and in good humour	Joking at inappropriate times
	Bragging; showing off; talking only about self
Expressing genuine interest in the other person	Monopolizing the conversation
Giving others a chance to express their views or share information	Interrupting
	Showing obvious disinterest
Listening attentively; hearing other person out	Keeping a sour facial expression
Sharing one's self with others; smiling; greeting others	Withholding customary social cues such as greetings, nods, 'uh-huh' and the like
Giving positive non-verbal messages of acceptance and respect for others	Throwing verbal barbs at others
	Using non-verbal put-downs
Praising and complimenting others sincerely	Insulting and otherwise verbally abusing others
Expressing respect for the values and opinions of others	Speaking dogmatically; not respecting others' opinions
Giving suggestions constructively	Complaining or whining excessively
Compromising; negotiating; helping others to succeed	Criticising excessively; fault finding
	Demanding one's own way; refusing to negotiate or compromise
	Ridiculing others
	Patronising and talking down to others

LOW-STRESS COMMUNICATION

Helping employees and colleagues to keep their own stress levels down will help you to keep yours down. It will also help everyone to work more productively if low-stress communication techniques are adopted.

GOOD PRACTICE

A staff development time should be devoted to working harmoniously. See the list of rules for low stress working on pages 137–138.

A good rule of thumb is to try to make as many of your transactions as you can relatively rewarding and positive for the other person. Of course, this is not always possible because of the nature of some kinds of problems, because some other people may lack the social skills necessary to cooperate in making transactions positive and because you occasionally need to take a strong position in opposition to others. However, over the course of your many transactions with your employees and your colleagues, you should be able to make the great majority of transactions go smoothly and comfortably.

This would seem such an obvious point as not to deserve mentioning if it were not for the fact that so many people who work together in organisations do not seem to grasp it at all. Many others can keep it in mind only under pleasant circumstances but lose their grip on it when the pressure is on.

Relatively few managers seem to have developed the skill of putting others at ease and helping them stay there through the course of a business transaction, especially one that presents difficulties for them.

Think of your own personal communicating style as being either punishing or rewarding for others according to their individual reactions to the ways in which you treat them. You can assess this quite simply by studying their behaviour toward you. In behavioural science terms a punishing experience is one an individual is not likely to repeat; a rewarding experience is one he is likely to want to have again. This means that, if the people with whom you are communicating usually experience their transactions with you as positive, affirming to their own self-esteem, and productive for them personally, *they will usually come back for more*. If they do not like the results, *they will tend to interact with you as little as possible*. This principle provides a very simple way to assess your communicating skills and to inventory the specific managerial behaviour that causes stress in others as well as that which helps them reduce stress.

Management of stress in staff

The hindrance to change list below reads like a straightforward list of stress symptoms. This is for the very good reason that stress for some is not only caused by change, but individuals already suffering stress from other sources find change more threatening and distressing than others.

A MNEMONIC IDENTIFYING HINDRANCES TO CHANGE

C Conflict/cynicism
O Obfuscation
F Fatigue
F Frustration
E Envy
E Ennui (resistance through lack of interest)

GOOD PRACTICE

It is the role of the manager to identify possible origins of stress in staff members and to prevent their condition affecting the working of the nursery and particularly the lives of the parents, who in their turn are also dealing with life events and other stressors.

STRESS AT WORK

Change is not the only source of stress at work. The following factors will also be influential:

1. Poorly defined jobs, tasks, responsibilities, and ranges of authority in the nursery
2. Prior history of conflict between two or more people or groups of people, e.g. staff of baby room versus those of toddler room
3. Interdepartmental relationships that frequently place members at cross purposes; tradition adversary relationships such as nursery staff versus teachers, administration versus social work
4. Unreasonable levels of pressure and pace in the organisation – this refers back to change but could also be a function of staff shortage
5. Severe economic downturn that jeopardises the job security of organisation members
6. Overly competitive climate fostered by top management and managers at various levels
7. Favouritism shown by managers to one or two employees
8. Punitive, accusative or threatening style of treatment by a unit manager, leading to escapist behaviour such as blaming others and shifting responsibility
9. Unclear or arbitrary standards for advancement and promotion in the organisation; inconsistent patterns of reward
10. Lack of support in liaison with parents/carers or outside agencies.

Activity
Using the above list of ten items and this text as a resource find guidance on tackling each item. Work in twos if you find it helpful to discuss each area.

STRESS IN GENERAL

Stress has no one definition. However, Selye (1956) tells us it is the 'non-specific response of the body to any demand made on it'. This is commonly thought of as the *physiological model of stress.*

In this school of thought, fathered by Hans Selye, it is maintained that in order to cope with the physiological aspects of stress one must know how the body reacts to stressful situations. Only by using this knowledge can the stress coping mechanisms be put in place.

The physiological effects of stress (see the diagram below) are:

- stored sugar and fats pour into the bloodstream to provide fuel for quick energy
- the breathing rate shoots up, providing more oxygen
- red blood cells flood the bloodstream, carrying more oxygen to the muscles of the limbs and to the brain

- the heart speeds up and blood pressure soars, ensuring sufficient blood supply to areas where it is needed
- blood-clotting mechanisms are activated to protect against injury
- muscles tense in preparation for strenuous action
- digestion ceases, so that blood may be diverted to muscles and the brain
- perspiration and saliva increase
- triggered by the pituitary gland, the endocrine system steps up hormone production
- bowel and bladder muscles loosen
- adrenalin pours into the system.

These changes occur because of the basic nature of *Homo sapiens*. *Homo sapiens* is a psycho-physical being, i.e. the body and the mind are inextricably linked. If the mind is stressed or put under any threat; like the threat of redundancy, the body will respond exactly as if it were being physically threatened. The 'fight or flight'

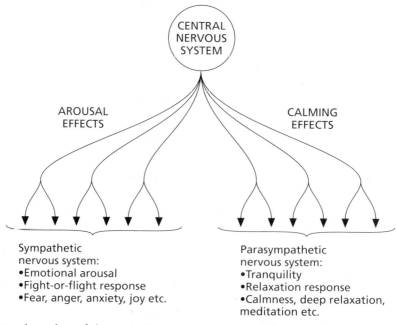

The two branches of the central nervous system work in opposition, alternately raising and lowering the body's excitation level (after Albrecht, 1979)

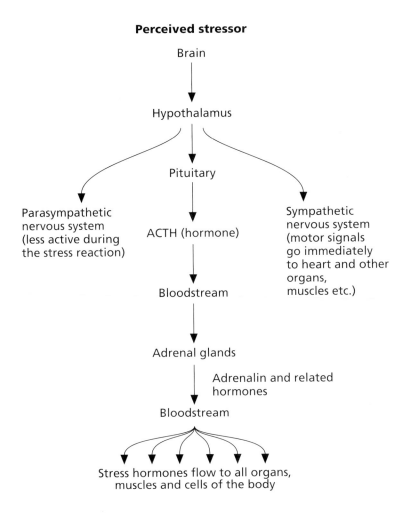

Perceived stressor

Brain

↓

Hypothalamus

Parasympathetic nervous system (less active during the stress reaction)

Pituitary

↓

ACTH (hormone)

↓

Bloodstream

↓

Adrenal glands

Sympathetic nervous system (motor signals go immediately to heart and other organs, muscles etc.)

Adrenalin and related hormones

Bloodstream

Stress hormones flow to all organs, muscles and cells of the body

The stress responses mobilise the entire body for 'fight or flight'

mechanism which allowed our ancestors to survive as hunter-gatherers will come into play and the body will undergo the physiological changes needed to do battle.

Selye, who was the most influential stress theorist, described three stages of the General Adaptation Syndrome (GAS) – the body's reaction to stress.

Stage 1: Alarm Integrated call-to-arms. Intense readiness and mobilisation of biochemical resources.

Stage 2: Resistance Vital resources applied to enable body to resist and adapt to the stressor.

Stage 3: Exhaustion Reversal to alarm stage in face of prolonged stress. Results in wear and tear, or death.

The individual experiencing stress will respond in one of two ways by the GAS model:

A enter stage 1 and progress to stage 2 and, assuming the individual copes with the stress, greater resistance will develop and growth occur, or

B enter stage 1 and, failing to cope by entering stage 2, move directly to stage 3 after which there is greater vulnerability and loss of resistance to stress in the future.

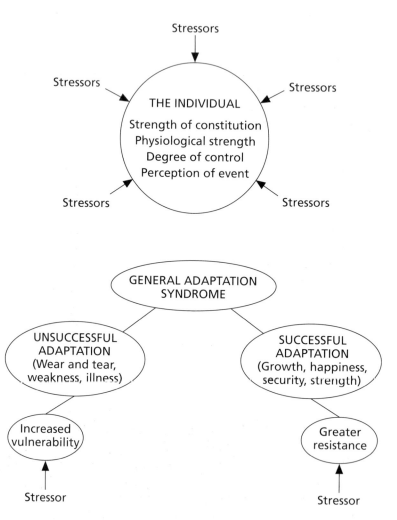

Summary of stress interactions

Knowledge of the physiological model of stress does undoubtedly help when taken in association with the knowledge of human development.

COMMON CAUSES OF STRESS IN EVERYDAY LIFE

Holmes and Rahe (1967) devised a list of *life events* – a social adjustment scale compiled by interviewing individuals who had just experienced a life-threatening illness. Their theory was that stress caused illness through a severe drop in the body's immune system. The drop was caused by the stress of a traumatic life event. They listed the events in the life of their subjects in order of their seriousness and the effect they had. This work is now treated as seminal to any study on life stressors and, although other researchers have adjusted the list, the principle is unaltered.

Activity

Use the Holmes and Rahe life event inventory below to check out your own stressors over the last year.

Give serious thought to this exercise because it will help you to structure your life and work in the future.

SOCIAL READJUSTMENT SCALE

RANK	LIFE EVENT	MEAN VALUE
1	Death of spouse	100
2	Divorce	73
3	Marital separation	65
4	Jail term	63
5	Death of close family member	63
6	Personal injury or illness	53
7	Marriage	50
8	Fired at work	47
9	Marital reconciliation	45
10	Retirement	45
11	Change in health of family member	44
12	Pregnancy	40

continued

13	Sex difficulties	39
14	Gain of new family member	39
15	Business readjustment	39
16	Change in financial state	38
17	Death of close friend	37
18	Change to different line of work	36
19	Change in number of arguments with spouse	35
20	Mortgage over $10,000*	31
21	Foreclosure of mortgage or loan	30
22	Change in responsibilities at work	29
23	Son or daughter leaving home	29
24	Trouble with in-laws	29
25	Outstanding personal achievement	28
26	Wife begin or stop work	26
27	Begin or end school	26
28	Change in living conditions	25
29	Revision of personal habits	24
30	Trouble with boss	23
31	Change in work hours or conditions	20
32	Change in residence	20
33	Change in schools	20
34	Change in recreation	19
35	Change in church activities	19
36	Change in social activities	18
37	Mortgage or loan less than $10,000*	17
38	Change in sleeping habits	16
39	Change in number of family get-togethers	15
40	Change in eating habits	15
41	Vacation	13
42	Christmas	12
43	Minor violations of the law	11

From Holmes and Rahe, 1967.
*Note: figures published in 1967.

The Holmes and Rahe work is very useful to the manager in forward planning.

GOOD PRACTICE

If a member of staff is moving house, it is not the time to be putting extra work her way. It is not sensible to move house, change job and get divorced in the same week, and it is truly amazing how often this situation arises.

Some stressors will affect everyone. These are known as *normative stressors*. They include congestion, excessive noise, toxic fumes and other things which are well know to cause distress to all people.

Other stressors are unique to the sufferers or groups of sufferers and these are known as *ipsative stressors*. Stress resulting from the fear of heights, water or spiders comes into this category.

As the GAS model illustrates individuals who have successfully coped with stress will grow from the experience.

CASE STUDY

'The typical case cited of the man made redundant in his forties who takes the opportunity to start his own business and never looks back.'

'The young nursing sister on the children's ward simply unable to cope with unsocial hours, demanding husband and young children who re-trained as a teacher, initially in order to accommodate the school holidays but who as a result, enjoyed a long and successful second career.'

Hence the adage 'from stress comes growth'.

However, the reverse is also true. One stress situation not accommodated leaves the subject weakened and less able to cope when the next trauma strikes.

In the case of work-related stress where the subject cannot cope over a long period, they will eventually succumb to the condition graphically described as 'burn out'. Burn out is a term used in both industry and social work to describe a state of apathy or ennui in which the subject becomes negative, detached and dysfunctional both personally and professionally. It is very poor practice if a child care worker demonstrating these behaviours is left in their post; it is both detrimental to the service and harmful to the children.

Management of stress in self

Activity

This activity is designed to enable you to develop rules for low stress working. Focus on work activities as a subset of life activities and develop a list of basic principles for working in a style that gets things accomplished with a minimum accumulation of stress points. Use the list below as your starting point, adapt and add to it as you see fit and review it from time to time. Use it to review and assess the balance between what you give to your work and what you get out of it.

1. In the course of doing business, build rewarding, pleasant, cooperative relationships with as many of your colleagues and employees as you can.
2. Rate your work by order of importance and manage your time effectively; don't bite off more than you can chew.
3. Manage by objectives, to capture the initiative on as many problem areas as you can (Albrecht, 1979).
4. Build an especially effective and supportive relationship with your boss. Understand his or her problems and help the boss to understand yours.

Teach your boss to respect your priorities and your workload and to keep assignments reasonable.

5. Negotiate realistic deadlines on important projects with your boss. Be prepared to propose deadlines yourself, rather than to have them imposed.

6. Study the future. Learn as much as you can about likely forthcoming events and get as much lead time as you can to anticipate them. Manage and plan proactively, not reactively.

7. Find time every day for detachment and relaxation. Close you door for five minutes each morning and afternoon, put up your feet, relax deeply, and take your mind off the work. Use pleasant thoughts or images to refresh your mind.

8. Take a walk now and then to keep your body refreshed and alert. Find reasons to walk to other parts of your building or facility. Greet people you meet along the way.

9. Make a noise survey of your nursery area and find ways to reduce unnecessary racket. Help your employees to reduce the noise level wherever possible.

10. Get away from your nursery/centre from time to time for a change of scene and a change of mind. Do not eat lunch there or hang around long after you should have gone home or gone out to enjoy other activities.

11. Reduce the amount of minutia and trivia to which you give your attention. Sign only those things that really require your study, understanding and approval. Delegate routine paperwork to others whenever possible.

12. Limit interruptions. Try to schedule certain periods of 'interruptability' each day and conserve other periods for your own purposes. Make telephone calls and return all calls at a certain time (except for emergencies, of course).

13. Make sure you know how to delegate effectively. Inventory a typical day's work and find out how many things you tended to do that could be assigned to someone else.

14. Do not put off dealing with distasteful problems such as counselling a problem employee or solving a human relations problem in your staff. Accept short-term stress instead of long-term anxiety and discomfort.

15. Make a constructive 'worry list'. Write down the problems that concern you and beside each one write down what you are going to do about it. Make a complete catalogue of current worries, so that none of them will be hovering around the edge of your consciousness. Get them out into the open where you can deal with them.

There are techniques taught to allay stress. Courses are available and much work on the subject has been published. However, the level of success achieved depends on the knowledge of physiology.

Relaxation as a stress management technique is taught on most courses and is widely available on tapes and videos.

Exercise and diet regimes are often recommended.

Assertiveness is also taught as a coping mechanism. The main strategy in coping with your own stress is to take charge of your own life, which is easy to say and hard to do. However, if you are physically fit, relaxed and assertive of your own needs, you are doing well.

Activity

This activity is designed to enable you to develop rules for low stress living. Study the list below and adapt it to produce your own list of rules for low stress living.

1. Make time your ally, not your master.
2. Associate mostly with gentle people who affirm your personhood.
3. Learn and practise the skill of deep relaxation.
4. Use an aerobic exercise such as jogging to build your health to a high level of conditioning.
5. Manage your life as a total enterprise, much as you would manage a corporation.
6. Do not become lopsided in any one area; seek rewarding experiences in all dimensions of living.
7. Engage in meaningful, satisfying work.
8. Do not let your work dominate your entire life.
9. Get your body weight down to a level you can be pleased with, and keep it there.
10. Form and keep sensible eating habits. Use sweets rarely, minimise junk foods and emphasise foods you like that are good for you.
11. If you smoke, stop completely.
12. Use alcohol only for social or ceremonial purposes, if at all; do not let it use you.
13. Eliminate the use of recreational drugs.
14. Free yourself from the chemical tyranny of tranquilisers, sleeping pills, headache pills, and other central nervous system depressants.
15. Free yourself from dependency on patent medicines such as antacids, laxatives and cold remedies by teaching your body to relax and normalise its functions.
16. Have an annual physical examination to provide extra peace of mind.
17. Jealously guard your personal freedoms – the freedom to choose your friends, the freedom to live with and/or love whom you choose, the freedom to think and believe as you choose, the freedom to structure your time as you see fit, the freedom to set your own life's goals.
18. Find some time every day – even if only 10 minutes – for complete privacy, aloneness with your thoughts and freedom from the pressures of work. Preferably do this for a few minutes several times a day. Maintain 'stability zones', personal rituals and comfortable patterns that insulate you somewhat from future shock.
19. Do not drift along in troublesome and stressful situations. Rehabilitate a bad marriage or else end it. 'Fire' those friends from your life who are not

really your friends. Take action to settle those matters that are troubling you. Do not leave troublesome situations unresolved for so long that they make you worry needlessly.

20. Have one or more pastimes that give you a chance to do something relaxing without having to have something to show for it.

21. Open yourself up to new experiences. Try doing things you have never done before, sample foods you have never eaten, go to places you have never seen. Find self-renewing opportunities.

22. Read interesting book sand articles to freshen your ideas and broaden your points of view. Listen to the ideas and opinions of others in order to learn from them. Avoid 'psychosclerosis' (also known as 'hardening of the categories'). Reduce or eliminate television watching.

23. Form at least one or two high-quality relationships with people you trust and can be yourself with.

24. Review your 'obligations' from time to time and make sure they will also bring rewards for you. Divest yourself of those that are not good for you.

25. Surround yourself with cues that affirm positive thoughts and positive approaches to life and that remind you to relax and unwind occasionally.

LEARNED HELPLESSNESS

The theoretical research which supports this work also gives insight into management stressors and suggests explanation of the executives illness.

This psychological study encompasses the notion that one will become 'helpless' when repeated situations occur in which one is powerless to act. A laboratory experiment was performed where two monkeys were harnessed together. Monkey 1 was able to respond to stimuli and, assuming he was adept, prevent both himself and Monkey 2 from receiving electric shocks. Monkey 2 could do nothing to help the situation and in a very short time he would accept anything that happened to him without resistance. He had learned helplessness. In every other way the monkey was healthy and thriving if not exactly full of initiative.

Monkey 1, the so-called 'executive' monkey, who was forced to take responsibility for protecting himself and his partner, was found on post-mortem to have severe gastric ulceration due to prolonged stress and anxiety. This experiment is often cited to explain the stress managers suffer because of the sheer complexity of their role and because they are taking it very seriously and feel the responsibility of their team and the need to provide for them.

The notion of learned helplessness is also used to explain the apathy of people in hostage situations and sometimes the depression of long term unrelenting unemployment. The work in this area is also very relevant for child care workers.

TIME MANAGEMENT

As stress is often associated with time pressure, time management is often used as a beneficial technique. It is concerned with being properly focused and able to accomplish your highest priorities. Management planning is the single most important factor in saving time in the nursery.

Most of us have had the dreadful experience of being busy all day but getting very little accomplished. If this happens frequently to you, you may believe that you have no time to plan. You must conquer this belief: once you have mastered a few techniques and developed some discipline in applying them, you will discover that you cannot afford not to plan. The time you take to organise yourself will pay off in a more organised nursery, fewer forgotten tasks and a more relaxed approach.

Before you can begin to plan, you must realistically assess the constraints.

- Some things *must* be scheduled during fixed periods. Work with suppliers, parents and so forth will have to be completed during business hours.
- Avoid planning anything for peak hours, such as dropping-off or picking-up times or children's lunch time.
- Some management tasks require certain environmental conditions in order to be completed effectively. If you are trying to do work that requires concentration, find a time and place where you will not be interrupted.
- Certain tasks will require the use of equipment – such as the computer – which is only available at set hours and this will limit the time periods in which you can do this work.
- Understand your own rhythm and work patterns; as you become better at planning your time this will come more naturally.

GOOD PRACTICE

Planning techniques will only work for you if you develop your own. Establish a regular planning appointment with yourself. This could be a once-a-week session (e.g. the last thing on Friday or the first thing on Monday), or a shorter daily session, or a combination of these. Schedule similar tasks together. If you have a number of letters to write or a number of telephone calls to make, try doing them all during the same time period.

Establish a regular 'quiet time'. Let other people know that you do not wish to be interrupted during specific times. Eliminate distractions from your field of vision. Place your chair so that you will not be distracted every time you see children and colleagues passing by – they can constantly distract you from the task at hand. Anticipate the things you will need (e.g. files, registration forms, copies of curriculum) and have them within reach before you begin work. Every time you break your concentration to find something else you need, you must spend time getting back into the rhythm of the work.

Do not insist on perfection in your planning. A system which has flaws will still be worth using. Work gradually with your faults. Effective time management can help you to simplify your life but only if you respect your own ways of doing things. The techniques you adopt should be adjusted to fit your own personal style otherwise they simply will not work.

Use the following ideas in order to keep paperwork under control.

- Do the work right after the task is given to you. Such instant action will fend off any tendency to procrastinate and let work pile up. You may have to refine your work later but, having started the task, you will find it easier to return to it promptly.

- Try to handle each piece of paper only once. Make a decision about the destination of each form, letter or circular the first time you see it.
- Remove sources of frustration. If you have to spend time tracking resources and gathering additional information before fulfilling an assignment, you are more likely to delay doing it. Gathering information makes the project seem more burdensome than it is. Try to get it in proportion: understand clearly all personnel and budgetary support available to you and where supplies and equipment can be found. Do not be afraid to request additional resources, supplies or guidance if you need them.

If the nursery is fortunate enough to have a secretary or an administrative assistant (or a share in one), you are way ahead in your struggle with time. A secretary can help not only by taking over certain tasks but also by helping you to maintain self-discipline and avoid panicking. Before a secretary can do this for you, however, you need to spend a certain amount of time together negotiating workable systems. Paradoxically, this is another burden on your time at first. However, investing time in training the secretary will pay off. If the secretary understands the nursery systems and why they are in place, then she (or he!) will do things in a way that is consistent with how you would do them yourself.

CASE STUDY

'In our nursery, if follow-up action is needed for a task, we make a note of it in the nursery main diary. For example, if we expect a reply to a letter from a parent in, say two weeks, we write "Follow up with Janet on ... " in the diary two weeks from today. If the follow-up will probably be by telephone then we have the number handy and write that down as well.

HUMAN GROWTH AND DEVELOPMENT IN ADULT LIFE

D. J. Levinson undertook a long term study of adult development using retrospective case studies and a ten-year observation period. It emerges that adults, like children, have *ages and stages.*

With the Levinson model, each stage has tasks that the developing adult undertakes. Some of these stages are characterised by change (transition) and some by stability.

The ages and stages that he identifies are as follows:

Early Adult Transition (Adolescence), 17–22
Moving from pre-adulthood to early adulthood.
Developmental tasks
1. Move out of the world of childhood. Change childhood relationships with family. Leave behind childhood peer groups.
2. Move into adult world and explore, test out some choices, e.g. choose first career.

Early Adulthood Life Structure, 22–28

Entering the adult world.

Developmental tasks

1. To explore a new world – travel – work out alternatives – find adventure, e.g. seek places of entertainment.
2. To create a stable life structure, e.g. find a partner.

Age Thirty Transition, 28–33

Becoming a 'real' adult.

Developmental tasks

1. To reaffirm choices already made.
2. To make changes (remedy 'flawed' decisions), e.g. start new career, new partnership.

Second Adult Life Structure, 33–40

Settling down to fully fledged adult life.

Developmental tasks

1. To make a place in society – have a skilled job, develop a family life, e.g. have children, make a home.
2. To 'make it' in the world – strive to advance – to be affirmed by the tribe, e.g. get a more senior job.

Mid Life Transition (Mid Life Crisis), 40–45

May not affect everyone to the same extent.

Developmental tasks

1. To question achievements/choices:
   'What have I done with my life?'
   'What am I getting from my job, my family?'
   'What do I want from life?'
2. To find a new path through life, or to modify the existing path, e.g. may now find a new partner.

At the end of this stage changes will have occurred – maybe one big crisis or many small changes or adjustments.

Middle Adulthood, 45–50

Building a new life structure.

Developmental tasks

1. To be less dominated by ambition/passion.
2. To be more bonded to others.

Age Fifty Transition, 50–55

Developmental tasks

1. To review decisions made at 30 and adjust these if they are flawed.

Completing Middle Adulthood, 55–60

Developmental tasks

1. To rejuvenate oneself, enrich life, e.g. maybe new home or car.
2. To achieve some fulfillment, e.g. successful children.

Late Adult Transition, 60–65

A period of significant development.

Developmental tasks

1. To conclude the efforts of middle adulthood, e.g. wind down working life.
2. To prepare for the time still to come (retirement), e.g. find new skills for retirement.

It is important to note that whilst each period may be flawed because of developmental work from previous periods that has not been done, each new phase offers the opportunity to change, adjust, modify, and to make better lives for ourselves.

The identification of where you, and also your staff, are in your life and career development and assessment of how well you are progressing with your tasks will allow a pattern to emerge and will assist you in taking charge of your life.

KEYS TO GOOD PRACTICE

- Be aware of stress symptoms and intervene if any member of staff is unable to leave them outside the nursery.
- Be prepared to keep an open mind about the change process.
- Be clear that sudden change is not in the best interest of the children and be prepared to argue for time to change in a responsible way.
- Encourage staff development around the need to take charge of your own life.
- Be sensitive to major events in the lives of staff and adjust demands accordingly.
- Be sensitive to your own needs, guard your own time and pace your work.

CONCLUSION

In concluding this book on good practice, we feel it is important to include a short postscript concerned with good practice in developing your own style and helping you towards a quiet assurance in your own work by adopting a few tactics.

As we have already discussed, there is no single right way of being an effective manager. However, there are many wrong ways. By including some or all of the following suggestions in your own management style, you are far more likely to become that effective manager, whilst – at the same time – also developing strategies for coping with your life outside work.

GOOD PRACTICE POINTS

- **Do not brood over things. Talk over your worry, everyone needs to do this at different times in their life.** Choose a friend, relative or professional helper you can trust – avoid choosing a member of staff in your own organisation.

Some results: You will have relief from strain and be more able to see what you can do about your problem.

- **Do not spend all your time on one issue. Escape from your problem, even if only for a while.** Lose yourself for a while in a change of scene, or an interest. There is no merit in 'sticking it out' and suffering.

Some results: Afterwards, you will be clearer-headed to come back and tackle your problem.

- **Being angry is allowed and even healthy. Use up anger by physical activity.** Channel your anger into a job that needs doing, clean out a cupboard or scrub a floor, or take a long walk or play a physical game.

Some results: You will 'let go' of your anger instead of bottling it up, which causes more tension.

- **Do not always insist on getting your own way.** Give in to others occasionally. This is easier on your nervous system in the long-run and you are the one who counts.

Some results: You will feel a relief from pressure and develop a stronger sense of maturity.

- **Be generous with your time and praise. Do something for someone else.** Even a smile or a generous word is a good start. Add to this daily.

Some results: It will help you to feel less isolated with your worry and to start to turn your thoughts outwards.

- **Do not take on everything at once. Deal with one thing at a time.** Select the urgent tasks first and get on with them; forget the rest for the time being. Tension and worry makes even an ordinary day seem unbearable. This need not be a permanent state.

Some results: This will help you to achieve something and the other tasks will seem easier when you get around to them.

■ **Do not expect too much from staff or yourself. Try not to be a perfectionist in everything.** If you expect too much of yourself all the time you can create a constant state of worry and anxiety. So decide which things you do well and put your major effort into these first.

Some results: You will avoid an open invitation to yourself to fail, and probably make life easier for yourself, and others.

■ **Do not adopt a judgemental approach to things. Try not to be too critical of others – or yourself.** Concentrate on other people's and your own good points and try to understand and develop them.

Some results: You will feel less frustrated and let down by yourself and others.

■ **Invest energy in team building. Develop co-operation with others, not competition.** Give the other person a chance. If you are no longer a threat to that person, he or she stops being a threat to you.

Some results: You will have less emotional or physical tension over reaching goals – real or imaginary.

■ **If someone is upset, do not stand on your dignity. Make yourself available to others – make the first move occasionally.** Neither push too much nor withdraw too much. Feelings of rejection and neglect are very painful but are often self-imposed.

Some results: At least you will know you have made an effort and this will build your confidence.

■ **Make the most of your private life. Plan your recreation time, however short.** Allow some time for a hobby or recreation. Unplanned time often becomes wasted time. Make variety part of the planning.

Some results: You will return to your work, or your problem, with a fresher outlook.

■ **If you are continually stressed, get some help – do not just suffer. Learn methods of exercise and relaxation and practice them daily.** You are aiming to be in control of your body and learning how to counteract tension and anxiety.

Some results: You will unlock tension in every part of your body and even prevent tension in the future.

APPENDIX A: SAMPLES

How to use this section

On the following pages there is a series of samples of the kind of policies, procedures, forms and statements of good practice which might exist in any nursery.

Each sample refers to an aspect of the work of the nursery manager, as covered in the text of the book. The reference to each sample is marked in an 'In the nursery' feature within the relevant chapter and each sample also has a reference to its corresponding text.

The samples do not cover every event for which a form or other document may be needed, nor are they the most perfect examples of their kind in existence. They are included as examples of the sort of thing that may be required. They are reproduced so that they can be easily used by the staff team in the nursery as a model – a starting point – from which their own policies, procedures and practices can be devised.

The samples are not intended to be used in their current format but to be amended by nursery staff to meet the needs of their own organisation.

Contents

SECTION FOUR PROCESSES FOR REVIEWING CHILDREN'S DEVELOPMENT

SECTION FIVE PROCESSES FOR STAFFING

SAMPLE 1

Mission Statement

The context in which this sample is to be used is described on page 49.

This is an example of a Mission Statement for a nursery called Nicetown Nursery. If your staff team wish to write a mission statement for your centre, this could be used as a model.

Nicetown Nursery is a community facility providing places for children (aged 2 to 5 years) on a first come, first served basis. The nursery will be open at times to meet the needs of working parents. Places within the nursery will be available primarily to children who live in Nicetown Borough. If there are any spare places, these will be available to children whose parents/carers work in the borough.

SAMPLE 2

Policy statements on equal opportunities

The context in which this sample is to be used is described on page 50.

An Equal Opportunities Policy is required under the 1989 Children Act. We give two different sample policies, either of which could be used as a model for your nursery.

POLICY A

The Nursery recognises and welcomes all legislation and existing codes of practice produced by the appropriate Commissions for the promotion of equal opportunities for all.

The Nursery aims to ensure that individuals are recruited, selected, trained and promoted on the basis of occupational skill requirements. In this respect, the Nursery will ensure that no job applicant or employee will receive less favourable treatment on the grounds of age, gender, marital status, race, religion, colour, cultural or national origin or sexuality, which cannot be justified as being necessary for the safe and effective performance of the work or training for the work.

This policy is brought to the attention of every employee and applicant and user.

POLICY B

We believe that good child care is, by definition, non-sexist and that the elimination of sexism will benefit all children.

The Nursery and our staff are committed to:
Users are encouraged to:
1. Encourage positive role models, displayed through toys, imaginary play etc., that promote non-stereotyped images. Books will also be selected to promote such images of both men and women, boys and girls.
2. All children will be encouraged to join in all activities, i.e. dressing up, shop, home corner, dolls, climbing on large apparatus, bikes etc.
3. Regularly review our child care practice to remove those practices which discriminate unfairly on the grounds of gender.
4. We acknowledge that pre-conceptions relating to gender and sexism are abundant within language and will challenge such language where appropriate.

SAMPLE 3

Policy statement on health and safety

The context in which this sample is to be used is described on page 51.

A Health and Safety Policy is required under the 1989 Children Act. We give two different sample policies, either of which could be used as a model for your nursery.

POLICY A

HEALTH AND SAFETY POLICY

All Health and Safety documents must at all times be available for inspection.
a. No smoking on the premises.
b. No hot drinks in any room occupied by a child/children.
c. No inappropriate jewellery to be worn. One pair of stud earrings and a wedding ring is acceptable.
d. Dress code: smart and practical with sensible shoes.
e. No running inside the premises.
f. Children should be encouraged to run outside in a safe environment.
g. All electrical sockets should be protected by safety plugs, no trailing wires.
h. All cleaning materials/toilet cleaner to be placed out of the reach of children.
i. All fire exits to be clearly marked and free from obstruction.
j. All fire extinguishers to be clearly labelled.
k. A copy of the fire drill should be clearly visible at fire exits.
l. Protective clothing shall be worn when serving food.
m. Never leave scissors or potentially dangerous objects lying within reach of children.
n. Nuts, e.g. peanuts, are not allowed in the Nursery.
o. Any accident involving body fluid must be reported to the Senior First Aider on duty.
p. Telephone calls must be received before 8 a.m. if a member of staff is not well enough to attend work. This includes all gastric problems and high temperatures.
q. All staff should familiarise themselves with the First Aid Cabinet.
r. The appointed First Aider must carry disposable gloves and tissues in the garden.
s. No pills or medication to be administered by the Management.
t. Only qualified Nursery Nurses or Nurses are allowed to administer medicine to a child.
u. No student should be left unsupervised at any time, and children must be supervised at all times.
v. Under no circumstances may a member of staff take a child from the Nursery unless written consent has been obtained from the parent of the named child.

POLICY B

AIMS AND OBJECTIVES

The aim of this policy statement is to ensure that all reasonably practical steps are taken to ensure the health, safety and welfare of all persons using the premises. To achieve this we will actively work towards the following objectives:

a. To establish and maintain a safe and healthy environment throughout the Nursery.

b. To establish and maintain safe working procedures amongst staff and children.

c. To make arrangements for ensuring safety and the absence of risks to health in connection with the use, handling, storage and transport of articles and substances.

d. To ensure the provision of sufficient information, instruction and supervision to enable all people working in or using the Nursery to avoid hazards and contribute positively to their own safety and health at work and to ensure that they have access to health and safety training as and when provided.

e. To maintain a safe and healthy place of work and safe access and egress from it.

f. To formulate effective procedures for use in case of fire and other emergencies and for evacuating the Nursery premises.

g. To follow the regulations of the Health & Safety at Work Act 1974 and any other relevant legislation.

SAMPLE 4

Policy statement on parents as partners

The context in which this sample is to be used is described on page 51.

A Parents-as-Partners Policy is required under the 1989 Children Act. Because this may sometimes be a sensitive issue, we give three different sample policies which can be used as models.

POLICY A

PARENTS AS PARTNERS: STATEMENT OF POLICY

The nursery team will work with parents as partners in providing quality care for their children.

1. All parents will be welcome to visit the Nursery at any time.
2. Parents will have access to their child's records and will be consulted in respect to the care given.
3. Parents will be invited to send representatives to form a Nursery Management Committee.
4. A suggestion system will be put into operation.
5. Parents will be given a copy of all the Policies of the Nursery.
6. Parent groups will be accorded hospitality and all facilities on the Nursery premises.

POLICY B

POLICY STATEMENT ON PARENTAL PARTICIPATION

It is the policy of the Nursery to ensure that parents/carers have the opportunity to actively participate, at all levels, as partners, in the policy/decision-making process of the organisation and in the planning and delivery of services to their children. Through this we aim to enable parents/carers to feel comfortable in the Nursery.

The nursery aims to achieve this by:

1. Ensuring that staff consult with and seek guidance from parents/carers when planning and implementing child care practices.
2. Ensuring that parents/carers have the opportunity to work with their children alongside key staff in the Nursery.
3. Ensuring that parents/carers have the opportunity to review their children's progress on a regular basis with Nursery staff.
4. Ensuring that parents/carers are informed about the policies, procedures and guidelines of the Nursery.
5. Offering parents/carers the opportunity to participate in curriculum, festivals and all Nursery events.
6. Ensuring that parents/carers can meet with staff and other parents/carers to discuss relevant issues and concerns.
7. Ensuring that meetings are open to all parents/carers to come and observe.
8. Having a meeting each year at which the Parents/Staff Committee will be elected.

POLICY C

PARENTAL INVOLVEMENT

Parental/carer involvement is an integral part of the philosophy behind the Nursery. To this end the work is organised to allow:

1. Adoption of Policy Statement on Parental Involvement.
2. Open access at any time to parents/carers.
3. Parental/carer representation on the Management Committee.
4. The consultation of all parents/carers before the adoption/amendment of any policy statements.

SAMPLE 5

Policy statement on child protection

The context in which this sample is to be used is described on page 51.

A Child Protection Policy is required under the Act. Because this may sometimes be a sensitive issue, we give two sample policies which are widely different. Either of these could be used as a model for your nursery.

POLICY A

The Nursery has a duty to be aware that abuse does occur in our society. This statement lays out the procedures that will be taken if we have reason to believe that a child in our care is subject to either emotional, physical or sexual abuse or neglect.

Our prime responsibility is the welfare and well being of all children in our care. As such we believe we have a duty to the children, parents/main carers and staff to act quickly and responsibly in any instance that may come to our attention.

The Nursery has a duty to report any suspicions around abuse to the Local Authority. The Children Act 1989 (Section 47(1)) places a duty on the Local Authority to investigate such matters. The Nursery will follow the procedures set out in the Local Authority Child Protection Documents and as such will seek their advice on all steps taken subsequently.

1. Physical Abuse
Action will be taken under this heading if the staff have reason to believe that there has been a physical injury to a child, including deliberate poisoning, where there is definite knowledge, or a reasonable suspicion that the injury was inflicted or knowingly not prevented.

Procedure
a. Any sign of a mark/injury to a child when they come into Nursery will be recorded.
b. The incident will be discussed with the parent/main carer.
c. Such discussion will be recorded and the parent/main carer will have access to such records.
d. If there appear to be any queries regarding the injury the Local Authority will be notified.

2. Sexual Abuse
Action will be taken under this heading if the staff team have witnessed occasions where a child indicated sexual activity through words, play, drawing or

had an excessive pre-occupation with sexual matters or had an inappropriate knowledge of adult sexual behaviour.

Procedure
a. The observed instances will be reported to the Sub-Committee.
b. The matter will be referred to the Local Authority.

3. Emotional Abuse
Action will be taken under this heading if the staff team have reason to believe that there is a severe, adverse effect on the behaviour and emotional development of a child caused by persistent or severe ill treatment or rejection.

Procedure
a. The concern will be discussed with the parent/main carer.
b. Such discussion will be recorded and the parent/main carer will have access to such records.
c. If there appear to be any queries regarding the circumstances, the matter will be referred to the Local Authority.

4. Neglect
Action will be taken under this heading if the staff team have reason to believe that there has been persistent or severe neglect of a child (for example, by exposure to any kind of danger, including cold and starvation) which results in serious impairment of the child's health or development, including non-organic failure to thrive.

Procedure
a. The concern will be discussed with the parent/main carer.
b. Such discussion will be recorded and the parent/main carer will have access to such records.
c. If there appear to be any queries regarding the circumstances the Local Authority will be notified.

POLICY B

It is the policy of the Nursery to provide a secure and safe environment for all children.

It aims to:

a. Ensure that children are never placed in risk while in the charge of the Nursery staff.

b. Ensure that confidentiality is maintained at all times.

c. Revise staff awareness to Child Protection issues and procedures.

d. Ensure all staff are familiar with the local Child Protection Handbook.

e. Regularly review and update this policy.

SAMPLE 6

Aims and objectives

The context in which this sample is to be used is described on page 47.

Two alternatives are offered as examples.

STATEMENT A

The Aims and Objectives of the Nursery are:
1. To create a stimulating, caring and safe environment for ALL children in our care.
2. To actively promote the development of positive self image within the children.
3. To work as partners with parents/carers in an open and honest way.
4. To have an involvement with the local community.
5. To develop and maintain strong links with other agencies and for them to recognise our professionalism.
6. To create a non-sexist atmosphere by introducing appropriate toys, books and games to encourage equal development of both sexes.
7. To eliminate racism throughout its whole structure by:
   a. welcoming ethnic minority contributions to the policies and practice of the Nursery.
   b. providing positive images of different ethnic minorities and cultures, e.g. posters, toys, food, clothing, festivals.
8. A Keyworker will work on a 1:5 ratio with a group of children, monitoring their progress through 4 monthly Developmental Checks and a yearly Review.
9. By implementing 4 monthly Development Checks and a yearly Review, we aim to become shared carers and we feel that you should be aware of how your child is progressing.
10. To provide places for special needs children if appropriate, with staff who are trained to give the child and parent/main carer support.
11. To encourage the participation of parents/carers in all aspects of the running of the Nursery.
12. To encourage parents/carers to visit the Nursery at any time.
13. To provide an atmosphere which makes the child and the parent/carer happy and comfortable within the Nursery.

STATEMENT B

Aims of the nursery:

1. To recognise that the child's needs and safety are paramount and must override all other considerations.
2. To provide an environment that is not only safe but stimulating and happy.
3. To work in partnership with parents, carers and other professionals.
4. To take account of the children's needs arising from race, culture, language and religion.
5. To provide quality care and education for pre-school children.
6. To support the children's families.
7. To create a developmentally appropriate curriculum to meet the needs of each individual child.
8. To share information, resources and practical advice.
9. To formulate and encourage equal opportunities for both children and adults.
10. To support staff on training courses enabling them to develop skills and confidence through sharing full responsibility for their group.

SAMPLE 7

Settling in policy

The context in which this sample is to be used is described on page 51.

1. The Nursery staff will work in partnership with parents/carers to settle the child into the Nursery environment.
2. Once a child is accepted by the Nursery, arrangements will be made for a Home Visit by the Key Worker to the home of the child (this is to establish a relationship of trust with the child).
3. There will be a Nursery Visit arranged shortly after the Home Visit so that the child can familiarise him/herself with the Nursery.
4. During the first few weeks, parents/carers will stay with the child for sufficient time so that the child feels settled and the parent/carer feels comfortable about leaving her or him. This arrangement can continue until the child feels at home within the Nursery.
5. For the first few sessions, parents/carers may collect the child early if they so wish.
6. No child will be taken on an Outing from the Nursery until he or she is completely settled in.

SAMPLE 8

Behaviour policy

The context in which this sample is to be used is described on page 51.

Two alternative examples are provided.

POLICY A

1. The Nursery believes in promoting positive behaviour.
2. We aim to encourage self-discipline, consideration for each other, our surroundings and property.
3. By praising children and acknowledging their positive actions and attitudes we hope to ensure that children see that we value and respect them.
4. Nursery rules are concerned with safety and care and respect for each other. Children who behave inappropriately, whether by physically abusing another child or adult, e.g. by kicking or biting, or by verbal bullying, may be removed from the group. The child who has been upset will be comforted and the adult will confirm that the other child's behaviour is not acceptable. It is important to acknowledge that a child is feeling angry or upset and that it is the behaviour we are rejecting, not the child.
5. How a particular type of behaviour is handled will depend on the child and the circumstances. It may involve the child being asked to talk and think about what he or she has done. It may be that the child will not be allowed to make his or her own choice of activities for a limited period of time.
6. The child will also be asked to see if the person who was upset is all right and, if they mean it, to say or show that they are sorry. An immediate response of 'sorry' is not accepted if the child does not mean it, but is merely saying the word in the hope of being able to continue playing.
7. In extreme cases the child will be removed from the classroom or garden until he or she has calmed down and had time to reflect on his or her behaviour.
8. We need to give children non-aggressive strategies to enable them to stand up for themselves so that adults and children listen to them. They need to be given opportunities to release their feelings more creatively.
9. Parents will be informed if their child is persistently unkind to others or if their child has been upset. In all cases inappropriate behaviour will be dealt with in school at the time. Parents may be asked to meet with staff to discuss their child's behaviour, so that if there are any difficulties we can work together to ensure consistency between home and school. In some cases we may request additional advice and support from other professionals such as the Educational Psychologist or Child Guidance Counsellor.

10. Children do need their own time and space. It is not always appropriate to expect a child to share and it is important to acknowledge children's feelings and to help them understand how others might be feeling.
11. Children must be encouraged to recognise that bullying, fighting, hurting and racist comments are not acceptable behaviour. We want children to recognise that certain actions are right and that others are wrong.

By positively promoting good behaviour, valuing co-operation and a caring attitude we hope to ensure that children will develop as responsible members of society.

POLICY B

1. The Nursery believes in practising an approach which supports children's development of self-discipline. We believe that children who acquire the ability to be disciplined learn to balance their needs with those of others, feel good about themselves and become increasingly more independent.

2. Staff always treat children with respect. A child is never smacked, shaken or treated roughly. There are no circumstances in which such punishment can be justified. We do not believe that punishing children in any such form ever helps them to become self-disciplined.

3. The methods used in the Nursery will only be those which promote the development of self-discipline and will always be developmentally appropriate. They will be reflected throughout our whole Nursery approach.

4. Nursery staff are expected to model behaviour that they would expect from children. Furniture should be moved quietly when setting up activities/lunch etc. Careful consideration will always be given to the way that materials and furniture are arranged, ensuring that the layout is one which encourages appropriate behaviour. One example of this is to make sure that the water is located away from the books.

5. We are aware that limits be set in order to help children control their own behaviour. But, limits set will only be those that are truly necessary, because too may rules for young children are confusing and easily forgotten. The limits imposed by this Nursery will always be clear and a reason for the rule will always be stated. One example of a rule is: children will not be allowed to hurt themselves, other or things; it will be made clear that a child can hurt physically or emotionally.

6. Our approach will always be one that helps children to see the consequences of their actions. We will provide opportunities for them to learn how to interpret feeling, by listening to them and offering the necessary support that will enable them to verbalise their own frustrations, hurts and disappointments.

7. Children will know that they all have equal rights and that those rights will be protected, i.e. if a child is playing with a toy and another child grabs it, an adult will help them preserve the right to finish using it; the other child will be assured that he/she will get a turn later.

8. If a child needs isolation from others because of misbehaviour then the perpetrator of the incident will be removed; eye contact will be avoided. If there is a victim, then extra attention will be paid to that child. The isolation will last for a maximum of five minutes.

9. Our ultimate aim is that we will work in partnership with parents to lay foundations from which children will grow into happy, self-confident, well adjusted individuals.

A basic outline of practice guidelines
- Appropriate limits should be set for children and maintained consistently by all staff members.

Children need structure within which they can be free to choose and experiment. Unlimited freedom puts too much responsibility on children.

- Nursery staff should never say 'No' to a child without offering a reason or an alternative.

Children appreciate explanations of and suggestions for alternative ways to act, even if they appear to be ignoring them. For example, an adult might say, 'Don't climb on the shelves, because they could break or tip over. Maybe, you could build stairs to climb on with the bricks instead, or you could go and climb on the climbing frame.'

- Direction and commands given to children must always be followed up with actions. Children will only begin to trust adults around them if those adults do what they say.

If a member of staff reminds a child that he or she can cut with the scissors but not throw them, and if they are thrown they will be taken away, this 'promise' must be kept.

Consistent follow-through will eventually make a child realise that staff mean business and that they will keep their promises and commands.

- Staff should never shout at children, raising the intonation of the voice will generally make a child take notice.

SAMPLE 9

Food management policy

The context in which this sample is to be used is described on page 51.

AIMS

The Nursery will adopt a Policy that will ensure that the standards of table manners and behaviour which is expected will be consistent.

Meal times should be a happy, social occasion for staff and children alike.

GENERAL PROCEDURES

1. Individual dietary requirements will be respected.
2. If a child does not finish his first course he will be given a small helping of dessert.
3. Staff will set a good example of good table manners.
4. Cultural differences in eating habits will be respected.
5. Children will be encouraged to say 'Please' and 'Thank you' and to sit still.
6. Children will be encouraged to wait before starting their meal until all the others have been served.
7. Conversation will be encouraged, but no shouting.
8. Any child who shows signs of distress will have his food removed without any fuss.
9. Children not on special diets will be encouraged to eat a small piece of everything.
10. Staff will set a good example by eating the same food as the children.
11. Children who are slow eaters will be given time and not rushed.
12. Quantities will take account of the ages of the children.
13. Children will be encouraged, where reasonably possible, to wait until everybody has finished before starting on their sweet.
14. Menus will be displayed for parents to see.

SAMPLE 10

Policy statement on the integration of children with special needs

The context in which this sample is to be used is described on page 51.

The school is committed to the integration of children with special needs. Our philosophy is that children with a special need have a right to be educated and to develop to their full potential alongside other children. Everyone stands to gain if all children are allowed to share the same opportunities and helped to overcome any disadvantages they may have to face.

How will integration be achieved?

(a) *Access*

1. Wide doors are available for wheelchairs.
2. The entrance to the Nursery is ramped.
3. The play area is on one level.
4. Suitable bathroom, toilet and changing facilities are available.
5. We will assess each child's needs in terms of access and adapt our facilities as appropriate.

(b) *Support and expertise*

1. There are several members of the staff team who are experienced in the care of children with special needs.
2. Outside agencies, including the Health and Education Authorities, will be called on to give advice and support and the staff team will receive training where appropriate.
3. Staff will work together with parents/main carers as partners to give day to day care for the child and parents/carers will be given support by all the staff team.
4. We ensure that all children are treated as equals and are encouraged to take part in every aspect of the Nursery activities. All children will be involved in the daily routine, e.g. garden, music and movement, routine visits to the shops. When outings are being organised, children with special needs will always be included.
5. Wherever possible we will promote positive images of those with special needs.

SAMPLE 11

Policy statement on race and culture

The context in which this sample is to be used is described on page 51.

The Nursery believes that it is the right of every worker and user (both adult and child) to be treated as an equal and with respect, and that no religion or culture is inherently superior to any other.

The Nursery will not tolerate racism in any form.

The Nursery and our staff are committed to:

Users are encouraged to:

1. Promote positive role models.
2. Actively promote equal opportunities at all times.
3. Challenge those (including children) who do not do so.
4. Challenge any form of racial abuse and report any incidents of this to the Manager who will report to the Management Committee where appropriate.
5. All staff will be continually reviewing their working practice and relationships in order to provide the best service to all Nursery users.
6. All toys and books etc. will be selected in order to provide positive images.
7. The Nursery acknowledges the diversity of religious practices, customs and festivals and will provide opportunities for all users to share in these whenever possible.

SAMPLE 12

Complaints procedure

The context in which this sample is to be used is described on page 54.

If a parent/carer has an issue either involving their individual child or the Nursery as a whole, they should in the first instance raise this issue with either their child's Keyworker or the Manager of the Nursery. If the parent/carer feels unable or unwilling to raise the matter in this way, they can approach either:

a. the Parent Representatives on the Management Committee; or

b. the Chair or Honorary Secretary of the Association.

In the first instance every effort will be made to resolve any matters within the setting of the Nursery.

Issues raised will be dealt with within the following appropriate framework:

a. A matter relating to an individual child should be discussed between the parent/ carer and the Manager.

b. Should the matter not be resolved, the issue will be brought to the attention of the Management Committee who will meet with all parties involved.

c. Issues surrounding individual children should not be raised formally with Parent Representatives, but if the circumstances are appropriate the parent/carer may formally approach the Officers of the Management Committee.

d. Should the matter still remain unresolved, it will be raised with the Management Committee.

e. If the matter raised concerns a general or policy issue, again it should first be raised with the Manager of the Nursery, who will report it to the Management Committee for consideration.

f. Should an approach on general or policy matters be made via the Parent Representatives or Officers it will be reported to the Management Committee for consideration.

At all points throughout these processes the parent/carer will be kept informed of progress.

SAMPLE 13

Accident procedure

The context in which this sample is to be used is described on page 54.

MAJOR ACCIDENT

If a major accident occurs the procedure is as follows:

At all times the staff *must* wear protective clothing (disposable aprons and gloves).

1. If able to be moved, the child is taken into the staff room and the Manager is notified.
2. She will then assess the situation and decide whether the child needs to go immediately to hospital or whether the child can wait for the parent/main carer to come.
   a. If the child needs to go straight to hospital an ambulance will be called. Then the parent/main carer will be contacted and arrangements will be made to meet the parent/main carer at the hospital. A member of staff will accompany the child to the hospital, but will not sign for any treatment to be carried out.
   b. If the child can wait for the parent/main carer to come, then the parent/main carer will be contacted and the child will be made as comfortable as possible and a member of staff will stay with them until the parent/main carer arrives.
   It will then be for the parent/main carer to decide whether to go to the hospital or not.
3. A report of the accident will then be recorded in the accident and log book.

MINOR ACCIDENT

If a minor accident occurs the procedure is as follows:

At all times the staff *must* wear protective clothing (disposable aprons and gloves).

1. The child is taken into the staff room.
2. The injury is assessed by Keyworker and if necessary the Manager is called.
3. The injury is then treated.
4. The child is then resettled back into the baseroom, and observed.
5. The incident is then recorded in the accident book and an incident slip is written and placed in the child's drawer for the parent.

SAMPLE 14

Exclusion procedure for illness/ communicable disease

The context in which this sample if to be used is described on page 54.

MINIMUM PERIODS OF EXCLUSION FROM NURSERY

Disease/Illness	Minimal Exclusion Period
Antibiotics prescribed	First 2 days at home
Temperature	If sent home ill, child must be off for 24 hours
Vomiting	If sent home ill, child must be off for 24 hours
Conjunctivitis	Kept at home for 2 days; thereafter until eyes are no longer weeping
Diarrhoea	24 hours
Chickenpox	7 days from appearance of the rash
Gastroenteritis, food poisoning,salmonellosis and dysentery	Until authorised by District Community Physician
Infective hepatitis	7 days from onset of jaundice
Measles	7 days from appearance of the rash
Meningococcal infection	Until recovered from the illness
Mumps	Until the swelling has subsided and in no case less than 7 days from onset of illness
Pertussis (whooping cough)	21 days from the onset of paroxysmal cough
Poliomyelitis	Until declared free from infection by District Community Physician
Rubella (German measles)	4 days from appearance of the rash
Scarlet fever and streptoccal infection of the throat	Until appropriate medical treatment has been given and in no case for less than 3 days from the start of treatment
Tuberculosis	Until declared free from infection by the District Community Physician
Typhoid fever	Until declared free from infection by the District Community Physician
Impetigo	Until the skin is healed
Pediculosis (lice)	Until appropriate treatment has been given
Plantar warts	No exclusion. Should be treated and covered
Ringworm of scalp	Until cured
Ringworm of body	Seldom necessary to exclude provided treatment is being given
Scabies	Need not be excluded once appropriate treatment has been given

SAMPLE 15

Procedure for preparing food

The context in which this sample is to be used is described on page 54.

All staff must remember to wash their hands before preparing food.

Breakfast – 8.00 a.m.
1. Bring in milk from outside and place in fridge.
2. Take blue freezer blocks out of freezer and place in cool boxes.
3. Wash and sterilise table top surfaces and other kitchen surfaces.
4. Lay tables for breakfast.
5. Lay out cereals, spreads and prepare toast.
6. At approximately 8.30 a.m., or when children have finished breakfast, clear table.
7. Wipe and sterilise all table top surfaces.
8. Wash up all crockery, cutlery and jugs.
9. Wipe and sterilise all kitchen surfaces.
10. Sweep and mop kitchen floor.

Lunch-time – 11.30 a.m.
1. Wash and sterilise table top surfaces.
2. Lay tables for lunch.
3. Lay out children's name cards, in key groups.
4. Serviettes to be placed on tables.
5. Prepare packed lunches.
6. Set up waste food table.
7. 11–11.30 a.m. main lunch arrives from meals on wheels.
   (if food arrives early place in oven)
8. All members of staff serving meal must wash their hands again, put on aprons and tie their hair back where necessary.
9. 11.30 main lunch time meal is served.
10. While children are eating their first course, dessert has to be served.
11. Fresh fruit to be washed and cut up, if a child dislikes dessert.
12. Clear tables.
13. Wash up.
14. Wash and place blue freezer blocks back in freezer.
15. Clean cool boxes.
16. Empty waste bin.
17. Prepare tea-time food.
18. All food must be covered and refrigerated where necessary.
19. Sweep and mop floor.

Tea-time 3.00 p.m.:
1. Wash and sterilise table top surfaces.
2. Lay tables for tea.
3. Serve tea.
4. When children have finished tea, clear tables.
5. Wash up.
6. Clean tables and work surfaces.
7. Sweep and clean dining room floor.
8. Wash out milk bottles and place outside.
9. Tidy kitchen.

SAMPLE 16

Procedure for bathroom routine

The context in which this sample is to be used is described on page 54.

1. Bathroom is to be cleaned morning and afternoon.
2. Toilets are to be cleaned with diluted disinfectant; toilet cleaner to be used around the rim.
3. Sinks to be cleaned with cream cleaner.
4. Soaps to be replaced when needed.
5. Toilet rolls to be replaced when needed.
6. Floor to be cleaned with diluted Flash morning and afternoon, *using bathroom mop only.*
7. Bin to be emptied daily.
8. Mirrors to be polished daily.
9. Window sill to be kept tidy.
10. J-cloths to be thrown away after use.
11. Toilets to be flushed after every use.
12. Gloves and apron must be worn when cleaning the bathroom.
13. Bathroom door to be kept open at all times.

SAMPLE 17

Procedure for laundry room

The context in which this sample is to be used is described on page 54.

Daily:
1. Flannels are to be washed daily.
2. Staff hand towel is to be washed daily.
3. Shower to be cleaned daily.
4. Sluice to be cleaned after use and disinfected daily.
5. Towels to be washed twice a week. *Wednesday* and *Friday*.
6. Tablecloths and tea-towels to be washed daily.
7. Bed sheets to be washed twice a week. *Tuesday* and *Thursday*.
8. Soiled nappies are to be put in a sealed bag and disposed of in bin outside.

Weekly:
1. Aprons are to be washed weekly.
2. Mop heads are to be cleaned in bleach weekly.

Monthly:
1. Floor mats and blankets are to be washed once a month.
2. Shower curtain to be washed once a month.
3. Dressing up clothes to be washed monthly.

General:
1. Nursery clothes are to be washed once worn.
2. Paint towels are to be washed once used and replaced in art cupboard.
3. Ensure cupboard is well stocked with:
   Disposable gloves
   Disposable aprons
   Baby wipes
   Nappy sacks
4. Wet clothes to be rinsed through, put in a sealed bag, and placed on child's peg.
5. Towel cupboard to be kept tidy.
6. Laundry door to be kept locked at all times.
7. Window to be kept open when tumble drier is in use.

SAMPLE 18

Procedure for animal care

The context in which this sample is to be used is described on page 54.

Rabbit and Guinea-Pig:
The rabbit and guinea-pig share the same cage. The hutch is kept outside.
1. Feed and change water daily.
2. Clean cage once weekly. (Ensure protective clothing is worn.)
3. In mild weather put out in the run in the morning, so they get some exercise, and place back in cage late afternoon.
4. Children are encouraged to handle the animals and help with caring for them, but ensure protective clothing is worn and hands are washed after handling.

Gerbils
We have gerbils, who live inside in the baseroom.
1. Feed and change water daily.
2. Clean cage once weekly.
3. Children are encouraged to handle the animals and help with caring for them, but ensure protective clothing is worn and hands are washed after handling.
4. The gerbils enjoy chewing things so paper toilet rolls or boxes are often placed in their cage.

Bird
The bird is kept in a cage in the baseroom.
1. Refill seed dispenser when it gets low.
2. Change water daily.
3. Clean cage once weekly.
4. Children do not handle the bird, as he is not hand tame.

SAMPLE 19

Financial procedures

The context in which this sample is to be used is described on page 59.

1. Resources
The resourcing of the Nursery is the responsibility of the Management Committee. The overall budget for the year is set by that committee. Financial monitoring of the budget is the responsibility of the Treasurer and reported to each Management Committee meeting.

2. Purchasing/replacement of equipment etc.
i. Purchasing of provisions (food) is the responsibility of the catering officer in consultation with the Manager and the finance for this will be via the monthly cheque administered by the Manager.
ii. The Manager administers a monthly petty cash figure of £50.
iii. The Manager administers the payment of Milk and Fruit bills via the monthly cheque.
iv. The payment of the Domestic is the responsibility of the Manager via the monthly cheque.
v. The Manager has the responsibility for ordering such replacement of stock (e.g. cleaning materials, paint etc.) as is necessary.
vi. The Manager can order new or replacement equipment up to the value of £100.
vii.Any purchases over £100 need the sanction of the Committee. In urgent circumstances, sanction must be obtained from the Officers of the Association.

3. Financial responsibility
i. The collection of fees is the responsibility of the Manager and/or Deputy.
ii. Fees must be banked daily.
iii. No fees are to be collected after Thursday morning.
iv. If arrears accrue, a formal reminder letter should be sent on the second week. If payment is not forthcoming the matter should be referred to the Honorary Secretary for pursuing.
v. On starting at the Nursery, a deposit of 1 week's fees should be collected.

SAMPLE 20

Nursery budget

The context in which this sample is to be used is described on page 59.

This is a typical list of nursery expenditure for a nursery of 22 children. Obviously the exact amounts will vary from nursery to nursery but the headings may be useful in planning your own budget. To complete the business plan you also need to prepare an Income list. Estimate how much income you expect to receive from fees, grants, bank loans, employer subsidy and so on. This will involve estimating the occupancy rate of the nursery (i.e. how many children will pay fees throughout the year) and deciding the financial policy in relation to fees.

COSTINGS (1995)	
Officer in Charge	£14,500
Deputy	£13,000
4 Nursery Officers (at £10,500 per annum)	£42,000
Employer's National Insurance (10.45%)	£7,263
Cook (30 hours per week)	£7,800
Cleaner/Laundry (20 hours per week)	£4,160
Employer's National Insurance (7%)	£837
Office Expenses	£2,000
Consumable play equipment (paint, paper etc.)	£1,500
Furniture and Equipment replacement	£1,500
Medical and toilet requisites	£1,000
Food	£8,000
Outings and Entertainment	£1,000
Staff training	£1,500
Insurance	£1,000
Advertising	£500
Audit	£600
Registration	£200
Total	**£108,360**
Total per child per year	**£4,925**
Total per child per week	**£95**

SAMPLE 21

Application for child care

The context in which this sample is to be used is described on page 57.

This application must be regarded as provisional and the booking of a place cannot be guaranteed until confirmation has been received.

Name of parent or guardian: ....

Address: ....

....

Telephone: ....

Name(s) of child/children: D.O.B.:

1) ....

2) ....

Ethnic origin: ....

Sessions required:

FULL TIME

Monday   Tuesday   Wednesday   Thursday   Friday

....

Work place of mother: ....

....

Telephone number: ....

Work place of father: ....

....

Telephone number: ....

Name of doctor: ....

Telephone number: ....

Emergency Contact Numbers:

1) Name of person: ....

       Relationship to child: ....

       Telephone number: ....

2) Name of person: ....

       Relationship to child: ....

       Telephone number: ....

3) Name of person: ....

       Relationship to child: ....

       Telephone number: ....

Please indicate if your child has any special dislikes (i.e. food/drink) or if she/he suffers from any allergies:

....

Does your child have any difficulties with
Hearing: ....
Sight: ....
Speech: ....

Please inform us of any relevant information which would help us enable your child to feel happy and secure at nursery (i.e. favourite toy, dummy, blanket, etc.)

....

I have read the details about the nursery and the contract for parents attached to this form and agree to comply with all the terms implicit in those details.

Signed: .... Date: ....

SAMPLE 22

Nursery contract with parent/main carer

The context in which this sample is to be used is described on page 7.

A fee is payable every week. On taking up a place in the Nursery you will be asked to pay fees in advance.

The weekly fee must be paid irrespective of whether your child is present or not.

Fee increases will be made on an annual basis on notice from the Manager.

Should your child have to give up their place in the Nursery, a notice period of 2 weeks is required.

Should the fees for your child's place be in arrears of more than 2 weeks, the Manager has the right to terminate that place. (Arrangements should be made to pay back any arrears owing.)

The Nursery opens Monday to Friday from 8.00 a.m. until 6.00 p.m. Children must be collected by 5.45 p.m. If any parent/carer has had 2 verbal warnings in a month about late collection, the matter will be reported. In all instances the Nursery should be notified that you will be late.

The Nursery will be closed on the annual Bank Holidays (lists of these dates will be displayed).

Parents must supply the Nursery with emergency contact telephone numbers and these must always be up-to-date. The parent/carer has a responsibility to notify any change of work place, home address or contact person.

Parents of children who are not potty trained will provide disposable nappies, although the staff team will give every support to toilet train the child.

Snacks and drinks will be made available to the child throughout the day and it is the responsibility of the parent/carer to notify the staff of any allergies the child suffers.

A hot midday meal will be available for the children at an extra cost (menus will be displayed for inspection). Parents/carers have the choice of whether to send in a packed lunch. No packed lunches supplied will be heated up. Notification, on a weekly basis, of the type of meal required must be made to the staff.

Any child who has been sent home from the Nursery because of ill health will not re-admitted for at least 24 hours. If a child is prescribed antibiotics they will not be allowed to return to Nursery for 48 hours. Should a child be on prescribed medication, it is the responsibility of the parent/carer to notify the manager or key-worker and to sign the necessary form consenting to administering of such. Parents/carers are asked to refer to the Illness/Communicable Disease List supplied for your information on minimum periods of exclusion from Nursery.

Parents/carers during settling in may stay until both you and your child feel comfortable and secure in the Nursery setting.

I have read, and understood the conditions set out above and agree to abide by them.

Name ....
Relationship to child ....

Signed ....
Date ....

SAMPLE 23

Invoice pro forma

The context in which this sample is to be used is described on page 59.

This is a pro forma invoice for nurseries to use when billing parents/carers for child care services. To illustrate this example, it is assumed that the nursery charges £10.00 per session (morning or afternoon) and there is a £5.00 charge also included for an outing, which the parents/carers had been notified of previously in order to receive consent. Good financial procedures include good management of cash flow, so it is important to state on any invoice when it is expected that the bill will be paid.

To be produced on nursery headed paper (can be handwritten or typed)

Date

To: *Insert name of parent*

INVOICE

Nursery services for *(Insert name of child)* for the period from
. . . . to . . . . *(Insert relevant dates)*

No. of sessions	@ £10.00 each	
	20 × £10.00	£200.00
Outing fees:	1 × £5.00	£5.00
Total		**£205.00**

Please pay in cash or make cheques payable to *(Insert name of bank account)*

Payment terms: For immediate payment.

SAMPLE 24

Financial reviewing processes

The context in which this sample is to be used is described on page 68.

1. The Manager and Deputy will undertake a full review of the operation of the Nursery every year in March.
2. A financial review of the operation will be undertaken each year as part of the budget making process.
3. The Manager has the right to ask the team to review any policy/practice at any time.
4. If a parent/main carer questions a policy/practice the team will review such and amend if necessary.
5. Reviewing working practice will be part of the supervision undertaken by the Manager with individual members of the staff team, as staff appraisal.
6. The Manager will report any changes to policies etc. at the Parents' Meeting.
7. Records of fee collection are to be kept as instructed by the accounts clerk.
8. Records of other financial transactions are to be kept as instructed by the accounts clerk.
9. The cash boxes are to be kept locked at all times and the keys kept on the person of either the Manager or Deputy.
10. Any financial discrepancies are to be reported to the Manager immediately.

SAMPLE 25

Checklist for evaluation of quality under-5s education

The context in which this sample is to be used is described on page 68.

Children are encouraged to communicate with others in speech.

They are encouraged to listen to a range of stories, poems, songs and explanations.

They are encouraged to commit some of the above to memory.

Children enjoy and share books.

There are a range of objects for children to sort, order and count.

Children are encouraged to use mathematical language.

Children handle two and three dimensional shapes.

They are encouraged to make and see patterns.

Children have interesting things to investigate.

They are encouraged to observe closely and describe what they see.

Their attention is drawn to happenings in the living and natural world.

They are encouraged to investigate items from the man-made world and discuss how they think things work.

There are materials and tools for children to make things.

Children are encouraged to notice features in the local neighbourhood, including people at work.

Opportunities exist for the development of physical skills: fine motor

gross motor

Children are given opportunities to express themselves through: drawing, painting, modelling, using malleable materials, dance, drama, music making.

Adults help children acquire simple techniques.

Children work and play together co-operatively and constructively.

Children relate positively to peers and adults.

Adults act as appropriate role models and are consistent and fair.

SAMPLE 26

Routine audit

The context in which this sample if to be used is described on page 79.

Play Equipment
Tick if provided

ITEM	0–2	2–3	3–5	Comments /Advice
WET SAND				
DRY SAND				
WATER				
PAINT				
CLAY				
DOUGH				
HOME CORNER				
DRESSING UP				
PHYSICAL PLAY				
BOOK CORNER				
TABLE TOYS LIST				
FLOOR TOYS LIST				
MUSIC/SINGING				
FINGER PLAY				
STORIES/POEMS				
OUTSIDE PLAY TOYS				
SCIENCE				
ENVIRONMENT				
ART				
CONSTRUCTION				
ANY OTHER				

Note: Keep this sample available for self-certification or 'light touch' inspection.

SAMPLE 27

Records

The context in which this sample is to be used is described on page 62.

All our records will kept on computer. Any parent wishing to see the records may have a printout.
1. Child's progress and development.
2. Accident records for children and staff.
3. Fire drills; cleaning schedules.
4. Safety checks.
5. Compliments and complaints.

In the event of a complaint, you should contact our Manageress who will be readily available to help you and answer any queries you may have. You may also complain to the Social Services Department, Anyplace.

As part of a multi-cultural society, we feel it is of utmost importance to promote respect for individual racial origins, cultures, religions and also level ability. Our Nursery will be available to anyone regardless of background. The toys and equipment will provide a positive self image of a multi-cultural society.

Displayed material

The context in which this sample is to be used is described on page 61.

Tick if displayed regularly

GENERAL

INSURANCE CERTIFICATE
FIRE DRILL PROCEDURES
MENUS – WEEKLY AND DAILY
POLICIES
CHILDREN'S PROGRAMMES OF ACTIVITIES
DISPLAYED INFORMATION
PARENTS' NOTICE BOARD
STAFF NOTICE BOARD

DISPLAYED CHILDREN'S WORK

ART
SHAPE
PATTERN
SCIENCE
MODELS
BOOKS

OTHER DISPLAYS

FINE ART
THEMES FOR CHILDREN'S WORK

SAMPLE 29

Daily routine

The context in which this sample is to be used is described on page 79.

Activities are planned in advance and we aim to provide various sessions from painting to craftwork, stories to music and softplay, all of which will encourage learning, together with free playtime. Each activity will depend upon the age group of the children and will encourage each stage of development from 3 months up to 5 years.

We hope to take the children on various outings throughout the year; full details of these will be available well in advance. As part of our commitment to ensure learning is fun, we intend to introduce monthly entertainment which will be amusing, stimulating and educating. All of this is to prepare the children for school and life. We are also looking at introducing computers into our Learn/Play scheme.

Note: Keep work based on this sample available for self-certification or 'light touch' inspection.

SAMPLE 30

Evaluation of nursery performance

The context in which this sample is to be used is described on page 54.

1. Liaison

Community   List

Agencies   List

2. Staffing

Establishment   List on Pro Forma include support staff

Please attach:
- Job Description
- Training/Development – Tick Pro Forma
- Appraisal/Discipline – Provide Written Account

3. Manager's Facilities   Office

Please Tick

Telephone

Clerical Support

External Support

4. Parental Involvement   –   Provide Written Account

5. Resources   –   Provide Written Account

Purchasing   –   Provide Written Account

Replacing   –   Provide Written Account

6. Financial Responsibility   –   Provide Written Account

7. Reviewing Processes   –   Provide Written Account

SAMPLE 31

Medication slip pro forma

The context in which this sample is to be used is described on page 57.

MEDICATION SLIP

Date: ....

Child's Name: ....

Parent's/Carer's Name: ....

Name of Medication: ....

Dosage or instructions of application: ....
....

I, the parent/main carer of the child named above, give my permission for the medication (named above) to be given at the stated times.

I state that the medication (named above) was prescribed by the child's G.P. and that the child has received the first 48 hours of the medication at home.

Signed: ....

SAMPLE 32

Calpol letter

The context in which this sample is to be used is described on page 57.

Dear Parent

As most parents are aware, children do get high temperatures at one time or another.

As we have a policy on medication, it would find be helpful if you could tick the boxes below that apply and sign the slip for us to keep in your child's file.

In a time of emergency when we are unable to contact a relative of a child in our care, we would like to be sure that it is safe to give Calpol.

NAME OF CHILD: ....

DATE: ....

MY CHILD DOES NOT HAVE AN ALLERGY TO CALPOL ❏

MY CHILD DOES HAVE AN ALLERGY TO CALPOL ❏

I GIVE PERMISSION ❏

I DO NOT GIVE PERMISSION ❏

for my child to be given Calpol in case of emergency.

Signed: ....

Name: ....

SAMPLE 33

Incident slip

The context in which this sample is to be used is described on page 57.

Date: ....

Dear Parent

Your Child ....

1. Needed a change of clothing because he/she:
   a Became wet playing with water/messy play
   b Had a toilet accident
   c Was sick
   d Was in unsuitable clothing (i.e. too hot/cold)
   e Other:

2. Was hurt:

....

....

....

....

Signed: ....

SAMPLE 34

Pro forma for review of child development

The context in which this sample is to be used is described on page 88.

Date: ....

Child's Name: ....
D.O.B.: ....
Doctor's Name: ....
Family Background (including place in family): ....
....

DEVELOPMENT
Language:
Messy Play:
Imaginative Play:
Concentration:
Hand and Eye Coordination:
Emotional Behaviour:
Gross Motor:
Fine Motor:
Self Help:
Socialisation:
Diet:

HELP NEEDED:
Decisions/plans made at review:

Present at review:

Signed (parent/carer): ....

Signed (key worker): ....

SAMPLE 35

Curriculum for the early years

The context in which this sample is to be used is described on page 88.

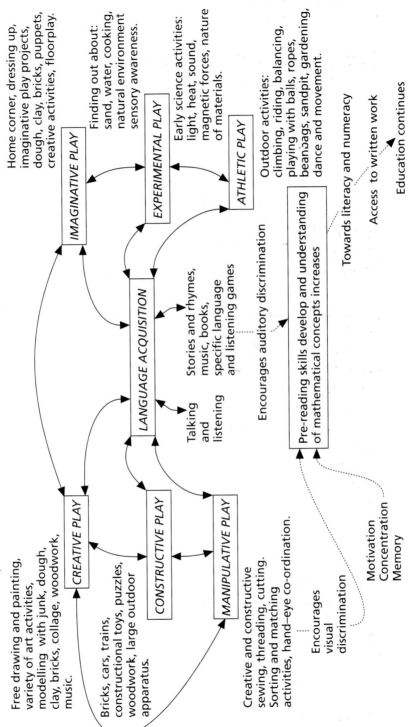

SAMPLE 36

Curriculum for transport theme

The context in which this sample is to be used is described on page 87

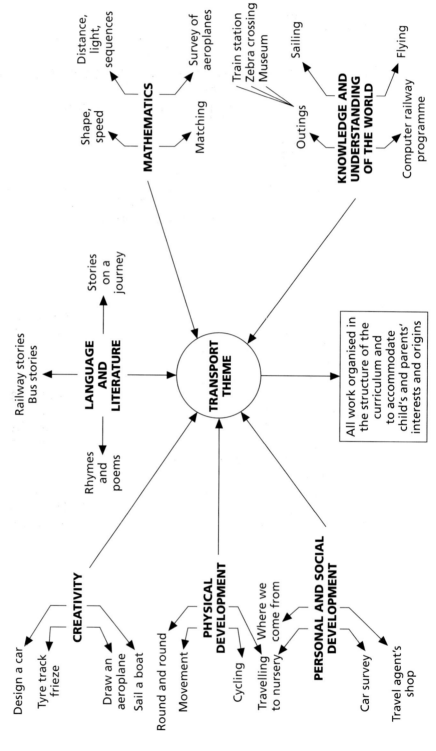

All work organised in the structure of the curriculum and to accommodate child's and parents' interests and origins

SAMPLE 37

Developmental review procedures (1)

The context in which this sample is to be used is described on page 88.

DEVELOPMENT MILESTONE
2 YEAR ASSESSMENT

Name: ....

A.O.A: ....   Key worker: ....

2 year Assessment	Average age	Complete
1. Walks easily on whole foot	18–24 months	yes/no
2. Mobility – runs, jumps, climbs	18–24 months	yes/no
3. Kicks ball without falling	18–24 months	yes/no
4. Linking words; vocabulary 50 or more words	21–24 months	yes/no
5. Spontaneous speech	18–24 months	yes/no
6. Builds tower of 6 bricks	24 months	yes/no
7. Makes circular scribble	21–24 months	yes/no
8. Recognises familiar pictures; turns pages singly	18–24 months	yes/no
9. Feeds without aid	18–24 months	yes/no
10. Dry by day	18–24 months	yes/no
11. Helps with dressing	24 months	yes/no

Language/Communication

	Muffled	Clear	Understood
1. Linking words			
2. Vocabulary 50 or more			
3. Spontaneous speech			
4. Understand simple commands			
5. Recognises familiar picture			
6. Turns pages singly			

Social Development

	Part	Fully
1. Engages in solo play		
2. Engages in parallel play		
3. Plays co-operatively with 1 child		
4. Plays co-operatively in small group		
5. Sits well at table		

Concentration

	Uninterested	Interested	Full
1. Builds tower of 6 bricks			
2. Holds pencil well			
3. Circular scribble			
4. Threads			
5. Puzzles			
6. Messy play			

Self Help

	Part	Full
1. Toilet trained		
2. Uses toilet on own		
3. Uses spoon/fork		

Can take off:	Yes	No
1. Shoes		
2. Socks		
3. Trousers		
4. Coat		
5. Jumper		
6. Dress		
7. Vest		
8. Pants		
Can wash hands/face		
Can dry hands/face		

SAMPLE 38

Developmental review procedures (2)

The context in which this sample is to be used is described on page 88.

DEVELOPMENT MILESTONE
3 YEAR ASSESSMENT

Name: ....

Key worker: ....

A.O.A.: ....

Physical Development

	Aided	Independent
1. Walks up and down stairs		
2. Runs purposefully and skilfully		
3. Rides tricycle		
4. Can stand and walk on tiptoe		
5. Throws ball		
6. Catches ball		
7. Uses bat to hit ball		

Language/Communication

	Muffled	Clear	Understood
1. Large vocabulary (infantile but intelligible)			
2. Can articulate clearly			
3. Asks questions			
4. Knows and joins in rhymes			
5. Follows simple commands			
6. Communicates with peers			
7. Communicates with:			
a. Family members			
b. Known adults			
c. Staff			
8. Speech is fluent			

Social Development

	Yes	No
1. Plays co-operatively in large group		
2. Child takes turns		
3. Participates co-operatively in group activities (singing, stories etc.)		

Self Help

	Dependent	Independent
1. Eats with knife, fork and spoon		
2. Dry throughout the night		
3. Uses toilet		
4. Washes self		
5. Dresses and undresses self and trunk		

Cognitive

	Part	Fully
1. Points to body parts:		
a. 3–6		
b. more than 6		
2. Names body parts		
a. 3–6		
b. more than 6		
3. Matches like:		
a. Colours		
b. Objects		
c. Shapes		
4. Can sequence		
5. Can sort objects		
6. Holds scissors correctly		
7. Cuts with scissors		
8. Can undo buttons		
9. Can do up buttons		
10. Holds pencil in palmer grasp		
11. Holds pencil in pincer grasp		
12. Draws a hair pin figure		
13. Completes a tray puzzle		

SAMPLE 39

Developmental review procedures (3)

The context in which this sample is to be used is described on page 88.

DEVELOPMENT MILESTONE
4 YEAR ASSESSMENT – Alternative A

Name: ....

A.O.A.: .... Key worker: ....

Physical Development

	Aided	Independent
1. Hops on one foot		
2. Stands and runs on tiptoes		
3. Walks up and down stairs adult fashion		
4. Rides a tricycle expertly		
5. Sits with knees crossed		
6. Throws, catches, bounces, kicks ball skilfully		
7. Picks up objects from floor by bending from waist		

Language/Communication

	Muffled	Clear	Understood
1. Large vocabulary (infantile but intelligible)			
2. Can articulate clearly			
3. Asks questions			
4. Knows and joins in rhymes			
5. Follows simple commands			
6. Communicates with peers			
7. Communicates with:			
a. Family Members			
b. Known Adults			
c. Staff			
8. Speech is fluent			

Social Development

	Yes	No
1. Plays co-operatively in large group		
2. Child takes turns		
3. Participates co-operatively in group activities (singing, stories etc)		

Concentration

	Part	Fully
1. Knows colours:		
a. Red		
b. Yellow		
c. Blue		
d. Green		
e. Others		
2. Counts by rote		
3. Understands concepts of 1, 2, 3		
4. Describes events seen in pictures		
5. Listens to and understands stories		
6. Copies circle		
7. Builds tower of 9 bricks		
8. Matches 2 or more primary colours		

Self Help

	Dependent	Independent
1. Eats with knife, fork and spoon		
2. Dry throughout the night		
3. Uses toilet		
4. Washes self		
5. Dresses and undresses self		

Cognitive

	Part	Fully
1. Points to body parts:		
a. 3–6		
b. more than 6		
2. Names body parts		
a. 3–6		
b. more than 6		
3. Matches like:		
a. Colour		
b. Objects		
c. Shapes		
d. Pictures		
4. Can Sequence		
5. Can sort Objects		
6. Holds scissors correctly		
7. Cuts with scissors		
8. Can undo buttons		
9. Can do up buttons		
10. Holds pencil in palmer grasp		
11. Holds pencil in pincer grasp		
12. Draws a hair pin figure		
13. Complete a tray puzzle		
	Yes	No
Can wash hands/face		
Can dry hands/face		

4 YEAR ASSESSMENT – Alternative B

1. Knows name, age and address

2. Climbs ladders and trees

3. Hops on one foot

4. Expert rider of tricycle

5. Builds tower of 10 or more bricks

6. Builds bridge of three cubes from model

7. Copies X V H T O

8. Draws house or face on request

9. Matches the names of four primary colours

10. Speech grammatically correct

11. Counts to ten or more

12. Knows several nursery rhymes

13. Can dress and undress

14. Eats skilfully using a knife and fork

SAMPLE 40

Home work feedback

The context in which this sample is to be used is described on page 97.

Date — Try and agree a frequency with which the work will be sent home, e.g. every Tuesday and Thursday.

Work set — Please be very specific about what the child is expected to do in performance terms.

Leave no room for misunderstanding. Include time to be spent on tasks if appropriate. Specify materials required.

Conditions — No distractions. Television off

With adult help/without adult help
Paired reading with another member of the family

Whether the work is to be given back to the teacher on completion

Parents' Comments — Encourage parents to be frank and honest about the activity.

This is not a judgement on the task the key worker has set but on its appropriateness to the child in the home situation.

We can all learn from this.

The parents tick the 'comments key' and also write something if they wish.

PARENTS' COMMENTS KEY	
My child did not understand what to do	❑
My child could not do this	❑
My child completed this task satisfactorily	❑
My child completed this task brilliantly	❑

SAMPLE 41

Goal setting pro forma

The context in which this sample is to be used is described on page 88.

FORWARD PLANS

Key worker: .... Date: ....

Short Term Goals:

Child's name	Goals to be achieved by next supervision	Methods used to achieve goals

SAMPLE 42

Job description: Manager

The context in which this sample is to be used is described on page 107.

The Manager will be responsible for the day to day running of the Day Nursery. The Manager will be accountable to the Management Committee of the Day Nursery.

Main Responsibilities
1. Ensuring a high standard of physical, emotional, social and intellectual education and care for children placed in the Day Nursery.
2. Supervision of and support to the other personnel within the Day Nursery.
3. The day to day management of the Day Nursery in terms of administration.

Main Duties
1. Supervising and supporting all personnel within the Nursery in their day to day duties.
2. Liaising with parents and other family members.
3. Liaising with the Local Authority and other professionals associated with the Day Nursery.
4. Overseeing the efficient upkeep of the building and maintenance/stock of equipment, furnishings and fittings.
5. In conjunction with the Management Committee, formulating and operating a programme of activities suitable to the age range of the children attending the Day Nursery.
6. Being responsible for all administrative duties associated with the management of the facility, e.g. maintaining records on the children and their families, ordering equipment, maintaining an inventory, keeping personnel records.
7. Being responsible for the collection, recording and banking of fees together with administering a petty cash budget.
8. Co-ordinating with appropriate agencies regarding trainee placements and supervising accordingly.
9. Convening/chairing staff meetings as appropriate.
10. Establishing and maintaining effective communications links with other agencies.
11. Attending monthly Management Committee meetings and reporting to ensure that all committee members are kept informed of current activities.
12. Working with the local community to ensure that the philosophy behind the project is fulfilled.

Qualities and Experience Required

We are looking for a person who is NNEB qualified or Teacher Trained (Early Years), with experience in working within the setting of a Day Nursery. A full understanding of the workings of such will be essential. An understanding of the philosophy associated with running such as a community-based facility will be an advantage. We are looking for a person who is able to work on their own initiative within a co-operative setting.

Salary and Conditions

Salary   *Give amount*
Hours   35 hours per week
Holiday 20 days per year

Applications are welcomed irrespective of sex, race, creed, disability or age.

Closing date: *Give date*

All application forms should be returned to:
Give address and telephone number

SAMPLE 43

Job description: Deputy

The context in which this sample is to be used is described on page 107.

Main Responsibilities:
1. To deputise for the Manager.
2. To ensure a high standard of physical, emotional, social and intellectual care and development for children placed in the Day Nursery.
3. To be responsible for any tasks delegated by the Manager.
4. To give support to other personnel within the Day Nursery.

Main Duties:
1. Overall management responsibility for the Day Nursery in the absence of the Manager.
2. Assist the Manager in providing effective day to day management of the Nursery.
3. Assist the Manager in collection, accounting and banking of monies and distribution of wages.
4. Assist the Manager in setting and implementing objectives and policy for the Nursery within the framework of the Management committee.
5. Assist the Manager in planning the training strategy for students.
6. To be responsible for the supervision of students, identify their learning needs and advise key-staff of these.
7. In conjunction with the Manager, to formulate, operate and evaluate a yearly programme of activities, following the guidelines of the National Curriculum, that is suitable to the age range of the children.
8. To be responsible for the day to day management of the baseroom, facilitating good practice by the staff team with regards to individual and group work with children.
9. To assist the Manager in promoting Equal Opportunities throughout the Day Nursery.
10. To work alongside parents/main carers of children with special needs to achieve full integration within the Nursery.
11. Identify the Physical, Emotional, Intellectual and Developmental, needs of children with Special Needs, and offer appropriate support, and relevant developmental opportunities.
12. Liaise with and support parents/main carers and other family members.
13. Liaise with the Local Authority and other professionals associated with the Nursery.
14. Attend monthly staff meetings and training sessions outside working hours.

15. Undertake certain domestic duties within the Nursery, i.e. preparation of snacks, cleansing of equipment.
16. Work alongside the Manager and Staff Team to ensure that eh philosophy behind the Nursery is fulfilled.
17. Undertake other duties as may be requested from time to time by the Management Committee.

Salary and Conditions:
Salary: *Give amount*
Hours: 35 hours per week on a rota basis
(8.00 a.m. to 4.00 p.m. and 10.00 a.m. to 6.00 p.m.)
Holidays: 20 days per year
Applications are welcomed irrespective of sex, race, creed, disability or age.

Closing date: *Give date*

All application forms should be returned to:
Give address and telephone number

SAMPLE 44

Job description: Nursery Nurse/Officer

The context in which this sample is to be used is described on page 107.

The Nursery Nurse will be working as a Key Worker for the daily needs of children between the ages of 2 and 5 years within the Nursery setting.

Main Responsibilities
1. To ensure a high standard of physical, emotional, social and intellectual care for children placed in the Day Nursery.
2. To give support to other personnel within the Day Nursery.
3. To implement the daily routine in the base room.

Main Duties
1. Formulate and operate a programme of activities suitable to the age range of children attending the Nursery, in conjunction with the Manager.
2. Prepare the children's records in your group and institute reviews for parents, in conjunction with the Manager.
3. Work alongside parents of special needs children to achieve full integration within the Nursery.
4. Foresee the needs of special needs children and give physical, emotional, intellectual guidance as appropriate.
5. Support all staff and engage in a good staff team.
6. Liaise with and support parents and other family members.
7. Liaise with the Local Authority and other professionals associated with the Day Nursery.
8. Attend monthly staff meetings outside working hours.
9. Undertake certain domestic jobs within the Nursery, e.g. preparation of snack meals, cleansing of equipment.
10. Participate in the training programmes of a wide variety of students (i.e. placements and volunteers), by giving guidance and support.
11. Work alongside the Manager and staff team to ensure that the philosophy behind the project is fulfilled.

Qualities and Experience Required
We are looking for a person who is NNEB qualified with experience in working within the setting of a Day Nursery. You will need to be flexible and enthusiastic.

Salary and Conditions
Salary: *Give amount*
Hours: 35 hours per week on a rota basis (8 a.m. to 4 p.m. and
10 a.m. to 6 p.m.)
Holidays: 20 days per year
Applications are welcomed irrespective of sex, race, creed, disability or age.

Closing date: *Give date*

All application forms should be returned to:
Give address and telephone number

SAMPLE 45

Job description: Nursery Assistant

The context in which this sample is to be used is described on page 107.

The Nursery Assistant will be working as part of a Key Worker team for the daily needs of children between the ages of 2 and 5 years within the Nursery setting.

Main Responsibilities
1. To ensure a high standard of physical, emotional, social and intellectual care for children placed in the Day Nursery.
2. To give support to other personnel within the Day Nursery.
3. To implement the daily routine in the baseroom.

Main Duties
1. Operate a programme of activities suitable to the age range of children attending the Nursery in conjunction with other staff.
2. Assist in the preparation of children's records and reviews for parents in conjunction with other staff.
3. Work alongside parents of special needs children to give full integration in the Nursery.
4. Support all staff and engage in a good staff team.
5. Liaise with and support parents and other family members.
6. Attend monthly staff meetings outside working hours.
7. Undertake certain domestic jobs within the Nursery, e.g. preparation of snack meals, cleansing of equipment etc.
8. Work alongside the Manager and staff team to ensure that the philosophy behind the project is fulfilled.

Qualities and Experience Required
We are looking for a person who is experienced in working with the Under-5s. PPA training is desirable although not essential. A willingness to undertake additional training is necessary. You will need to be flexible and enthusiastic.

Salary and Conditions
Rate of Pay: *Hourly rate*
Hours: $12\frac{1}{2}$ per week (at present we are looking for a member of staff to work 3.00 p.m. to 5.30 p.m. Monday to Friday)
Holidays: 20 days per year

Closing date: *Give date*

All application forms should be returned to:
Give address and telephone number

SAMPLE 46

Job description: Catering Officer

The context in which this sample is to be used is described on page 107.

The Catering Officer will be working within the setting of a Community Day Nursery for children between the ages of 2 and 5 years of age.

Main Duties
1. To be the budget holder for the provision of food and associated goods for the Nursery.
2. To be responsible for the purchase of such provisions.
3. To be responsible in conjunction with the Manager for planning weekly menus.
4. To keep weekly accounts of such expenditure.
5. To co-ordinate the serving of the mid-day meal.
6. To wash-up crockery and cutlery.
7. To be responsible for hygiene etc. within the kitchen area.
8. To prepare food for the tea-time snack.

Wages and Conditions
Hours: 12 hours a week (2 hrs a day Monday to Friday plus 2 hrs a week for purchasing provisions)
Wages: Hourly rate plus petrol allowance
Holidays: 20 days per year

Closing date: *Give date*

All application forms should be returned to:
Give address and telephone number

Issued: *Give date*

SAMPLE 47

Job description: Cleaner

The context in which this sample is to be used is described on page 107.

The Cleaner will be responsible for the up-keep of the above premises, which is a Community Day Nursery for children aged 2 to 5 years.

Main Duties
1. Empty and wash out bins in all rooms.
2. Tidy and dust Staff Room.
3. Tidy and dust Office.
4. Vacuum main Nursery room, Office and Staff Room.
5. Clean Nursery toilets, staff toilets and hand basins.
6. Wash floors in laundry, kitchen, bathroom and wipe out shower.
7. Wipe around surface in kitchen.
8. Damp dust where appropriate.
9. Keep a check on cleaning materials and re-order via the Manager.
10. Lock or unlock the building securely.
11. Undertake any other duties as may be required from time to time.

Wages and Conditions
Hours: 2 hours a day (5 days a week)
Wages: Hourly rate

Closing date: *Give date*

Issued: *Give date*

SAMPLE 48

Disciplinary procedure from staffing policy

The context in which this sample is to be used is described on page 51.

Detailed below are the stages that would apply to all members of staff in relation to disciplinary action for unsatisfactory work or conduct:

Stage 1 – Verbal Warning
The Manager will explain to the member of staff the reasons for taking disciplinary action, and discuss plans for overcoming the problem.

The discussions and plans will be recorded, and a reasonable time for review will be agreed.

Stage 2 – Written Warning
If it is considered, after the review, that progress is unsatisfactory, there will be a further discussion with the employee.

A further plan for review and discussion will be agreed and recorded. A copy will be sent to the employee clearly stating that any subsequent lack of improvement in conduct or competence may result in further disciplinary action.

The Management Committee will receive a report of this disciplinary stage, including a copy of the written warning issued to the employee.

Stage 3 – Final Written Warning
Should progress not be made by the time of the second review, a final written warning will be issued. This will specify a suitable period of time during which an improvement must take place. It will advise the employee that should they not meet the requirements specified, then consideration will be give to termination of employment.

The Management Committee will receive a report of this disciplinary stage, including a copy of the final written warning issued to the employee.

Stage 4 – Dismissal
If no significant improvement takes place in the employee's record after the preliminary stages of this procedure have been exhausted, the Chair of the Child Care Association shall notify the employee in writing of a time and date of a termination interview. Notification will be given at least 5 working days in advance and the reasons stated for such action being taken.

Detailed below is the action that would apply to all members of staff in relation to disciplinary action for misconduct:

Where an act of misconduct has occurred justifying consideration of summary dismissal, the employee may be suspended on full pay pending a disciplinary hearing.

Suspension from duty should normally only occur on the following grounds:

a. Where an act of misconduct has occurred of such a nature that the continued presence at work of the individual concerned is unacceptable to the Child Care Association.

b. To enable investigations into alleged misconduct to take place.

c. Where it is in the interests of the employee and/or the Child Care Association that the individual does not remain at their workplace.

Dismissal for misconduct cannot be implemented without the full knowledge of the Management Committee.

Any member of staff has the right of appeal to the Management Committee at any stage of the procedure outlined above and may be represented by a Trade Union Official or by a representative of their choice at all stages.

SAMPLE 49

Grievance procedure from staffing policy

The context in which this sample is to be used is described on page 51.

Any member of the staff team has the right to express a grievance relating to their employment. Detailed below are the steps that should be taken in this instance:

a. The grievance should be expressed orally, or in writing, to the Manager, who will attempt to resolve the issue at the earliest opportunity.

b. Should the grievance relate directly to the Manager then the approach should be made to the Chair of the Child Care Association.

c. If the matter is not satisfactorily resolved within 15 working days, the grievance should be raised formally with the Management Committee.

d. Any grievance addressed to the Management Committee should be expressed in writing and made available at least 10 working days prior to the scheduled meeting of the Committee.

e. In all of the stages outlined the member of staff has a right to be represented by a Trade Union Official or other representative.

If a member of staff has a grievance relating to a parent/main carer of one of the children attending the Nursery, they should not raise this directly with the parent/main carer.

In this instance all such grievances should be raised with the Manager, who will take any necessary action.

SAMPLE 50

Staff training and development monitoring form

The context in which this sample is to be used is described on page 117.

For each member of your staff, tick as appropriate.

	Taken	Available
FIRST AID		
HIV AWARENESS		
EQUAL OPPORTUNITIES		
MULTICULTURAL PROVISION		
CHILD PROTECTION		
NVQ ASSESSOR TRAINING		
WORKING WITH PARENTS		
LEARNING ACTIVITIES FOR THE CHILDREN		
MANAGING CHILDREN'S BEHAVIOUR		
RECORD KEEPING		
INDUCTION		
APPRAISAL		

SAMPLE 51

Preparation form for annual appraisal (1)

The context in which this sample is to be used is described on page 120.

This form must be completed by the employee and exchanged with the Line Manager at least 10 working days prior to the appraisal taking place.

Name: ....

Position: ....

Date of Appraisal: ....

Please list any duties which are not identified in your current job description
....

Please identify the areas of work in which you feel you have been most successful and why.
....

Please identify the areas of work in which you feel you have been least successful and why.
....

What factors have had an effect on your job performance?
a. internal
....

b. external
....

What kind of management support would you find most useful?
....

What kind of support from other departments would you find most useful?
....

Please identify any training you think would improve your performance and give reasons.
How would you like to see your role develop over the next year?
....

What would you consider to be reasonable projected targets?
....

Signed: .... **Dated:** ....

SAMPLE 52

Preparation form for annual appraisal (2)

The context in which this sample is to be used is described on page 120.

This form must be completed by the supervisor and exchanged with the appraisee at least 10 working days prior to the appraisal.

Name: ....
Position: ....
Date of Appraisal: ....

Please identify the areas of work in which you feel the appraisee has been most successful and why.
....
....
....

Please identify the areas of work in which they have been least successful and why.
....
....
....

What factors have had an effect on their job performance?
a) internal
....
....
....

b) external
....
....
....

Please identify any training which might improve performance.
....
....

What would you consider to be reasonable projected targets?
....
....
....

Signed:.. **Dated:** ....

SAMPLE 53

Staff appraisal form

The context in which this sample is to be used is described on page 120.

This form must be completed and signed by both parties within two working days of the appraisal date noted below.

Name of Appraisee: ....
Position: ....
Date of Appraisal: ....
Name of Supervisor: ....

Please describe any duties currently undertaken which are not identified on the job description for this position.
....

Please list the areas of work in which the jobholder has been most successful.
....

Please list the areas of work in which the jobholder has been least successful.
....

What factors have had an effect on performance?
....

What additional support will be requested from:
a) direct supervisor?
....

b) other departments?
....

c) management?
....

How will the jobholder's role develop
a. over the next year?

....

b. over the next two to three years?

....

Please identify training needs.

....

Agreed Targets and Timescales

....

Comments from Supervisor

....

Comments from Jobholder

....

Date of Next Appraisal

Signed: .... Supervisor, Date: ....

Signed: .... Jobholder, Date: ....

SAMPLE 54

Self appraisal technique (1)

The context in which this sample is to be used is described on page 120.

Structured writing linked to a job description (or list of key tasks)

This is an exercise for use in connection with self-appraisal. We have also provided 'checklists', giving advice on the issues raised. Each activity is free-standing, so that nurseries or day care centres can select whichever of the activities is appropriate. The activities can be done before appraisal starts or as part of subsequent training or debriefing.

1. Find a time of perhaps an hour when you can reflect without interruption about your work. You should aim for a quiet, relaxed and comfortable environment for this task. Then think about your job and how you feel it is going. Allow your mind to range freely over all aspects of your job with reference to your job description.

2. Write down your thoughts, commenting on how well your work is going in each of the major areas for which you are responsible.

NB. Sample 55 is a generic list of key job areas which could be used to support this technique. If you use this as a prompt, only use those headings which are relevant to your job.

SAMPLE 55

Prompt sheet key job areas

The context in which this sample is to be used is described on page 120.

The following general headings may prove helpful when analysing areas of responsibility.

1. **Nursery work:**
   Preparation of work
   Curriculum planning
   Managing the children
   Display work
   Liaison with relevant colleagues

2. **Child welfare and support:**
   Maintaining individual child records
   Overview of welfare/progress
   Liaison with parents/carers
   Liaison with outside agents – health visitor, doctor
   Liaison with other colleagues

3. **Administrative work:**
   Planning/setting objectives
   Maintaining appropriate records/documentation
   Organising resources
   Monitoring/evaluation/control
   Communication/interpersonal relations
   Staff development undertaken

4. **Other areas:**
   Links with parents/carers
   Links with the community/industry/other centres/employers
   Personal development/self-management
   Marketing

SAMPLE 56

Self appraisal technique (2)

The context in which this sample is to be used is described on page 120.

This is a useful exercise for any individual to go through before they have an appraisal interview with their manager.

Please respond to the following questions; write in note form if you feel more comfortable doing so:

1. Do you feel your job description is relevant?

2. Which aspects of your work do you feel especially pleased with?

3. Which aspects of your job have not gone as well as you would have hoped?

4. Are there any constraints or difficulties you are working under?

5. In what ways would you hope to develop your experience and strengthen your expertise both in the coming year and in the long term?

Name: ....

Date: ....

SAMPLE 57

Planning and organisational skills

The context in which this sample is to be used is described on page 120.

The following list of headings and statements indicates some of the important skills that all managers, no matter what their responsibility, are required to possess. The list is intended to help you to reflect on important aspects of your contribution as a member of staff. Look at the statements under each heading and consider your ability/effectiveness in relation to each statement.

	Experienced in/happy with	Keeping my eye on this	Need to spend more time on this	Not relevant/of immediate concern
PLANNING				
Perceiving your own group, department and centre needs in the short term/long term				
Setting and prioritising short term/long term aims and objectives				
Collecting necessary information before making decisions				
Drawing up a programme of activities to meet short term/long terms aims and objectives.				
Using the most appropriate methods to meet the different needs of individual children				
Generating new creative ideas, concepts and methods that improve the childrens day				
Making a conscientious effort to keep up to date with changes in child care				
Knowing your specialist area well enough to prepare adequately				

	Experienced in/happy with	Keeping my eye on this	Need to spend more time on this	Not relevant/of immediate concern

ORGANISATIONAL SKILLS

Adapting activities as necessary

Delegating tasks as appropriate

Managing time and money

Managing and using appropriate resources

SAMPLE 58

Follow up skills, communicating skills and fostering teamwork

The context in which this sample is to be used is described on page 108.

The following list of headings and statements indicates some of the important skills that all managers, no matter what their responsibility, are required to possess. The list is intended to help you to reflect on important aspects of your contribution as a member of staff. Look at the statements under each heading and consider your ability/effectiveness in relation to each statement.

	Experienced in/happy with	Keeping my eye on this	Need to spend more time on this	Not relevant/of immediate concern
FOLLOW UP SKILLS				
Monitoring/evaluating the effectiveness of activities				
Systematically checking on standards of work produced				
Insisting on high standards				
Accepting the consequences of your decisions and taking action as necessary				
Searching for methods to improve how things are done				
COMMUNICATING SKILLS				
Expressing ideas verbally/in writing clearly and positively				
Giving clear guidelines of what is expected				
Liaising with outside agencies, Health Visitor, social workers				
Being a good role model				
Providing information and advice to help others				

	Experienced in/happy with	Keeping my eye on this	Need to spend more time on this	Not relevant/of rimmediate concern

FOSTERING TEAMWORK

Being a member of/helping to foster an enthusiastic and productive group

Involving people in decision making/identifying goals to gain their commitment

Developing individuals to their full potential

Successfully facing up to and dealing with conflict using the most appropriate method

Accepting the responsibility to take initiatives/make decisions

SAMPLE 59

Relationships with people and professional development

The context in which this sample is to be used is described on page 108.

The following list of headings and statements indicates some of the important skills that all managers, no matter what their responsibility, are required to possess. The list is intended to help you to reflect on important aspects of your contribution as a member of staff. Look at the statements under each heading and consider your ability/effectiveness in relation to each statement.

	Experienced in/happy with	Keeping my eye on this	Need to spend more time on this	Not relevant/of immediate concern
RELATIONSHIPS WITH PEOPLE				
Assessing your own capabilities				
Seeing yourself as others do				
Encouraging openness and honesty in expressing feelings between individuals				
Recognising how and when your behaviour adversely affects others				
Adapting your own behaviour and attitude when they have a negative effect on working relationships				
Maintaining good self-discipline even in the most difficult situations				
Giving recognition whether in the form of praise or constructive criticism				
Treating people fairly				
Recognising the needs and problems of others by sharing concern and understanding				

	Experienced in/happy with	Keeping my eye on this	Need to spend more time on this	Not relevant/of immediate concern
Developing an atmosphere of trust and establishing a natural, comfortable and personal rapport				

PROFESSIONAL DEVELOPMENT
Being aware of and involved in planning and developments

Gaining from and contributing to group work and development programmes

SAMPLE 60

Team role questionnaire

The context in which this sample is to be used is described on page 112.

DIRECTIONS
For each section distribute a total of ten points among the sentences which you think best describe your behaviour. These points may be distributed among several sentences: in extreme cases they might be spread among all the sentences or ten points may be given to a single sentence. Enter the points in the table on page 241.

I.   What I believe I can contribute to a team:
   a. I think I can quickly see and take advantage of new opportunities.
   b. I can work well with a very wide range of people.
   c. Producing ideas is one of my natural assets.
   d. My ability rests in being able to draw people out whenever I detect they have something of value to contribute to group objectives.
   e. My capacity to follow through has much to do with my personal effectiveness.
   f. I am ready to face temporary unpopularity if it leads to worthwhile results in the end.
   g. I am quick to sense what is likely to work in a situation with which I am familiar.
   h. I can offer a reasoned case for alternative courses of action without introducing bias or prejudice.

II. If I have a possible shortcoming in teamwork, it could be that:
   a. I am not at ease unless meetings are well structured and controlled and generally well conducted.
   b. I am inclined to be too generous towards others who have a valid viewpoint that has not been give a proper airing.
   c. I have a tendency to talk a lot once the group gets on to new ideas.
   d. My objective outlook makes it difficult for me to join in readily and enthusiastically with colleagues.
   e. I am sometimes seen as forceful and authoritarian if there is a need to get something done.
   f. I find it difficult to lead from the front, perhaps because I am over responsive to group atmosphere.
   g. I am apt to get caught up in ideas that occur to me and so lose track of what is happening.
   h. My colleagues tend to see me as worrying unnecessarily over detail and the possibility that things may go wrong.

III. When involved in a project with other people:
   a. I have an aptitude for influencing people without pressurising them.
   b. My general vigilance prevents careless mistakes and omissions being made.
   c. I am ready to press for action to make sure that the meeting does not waste time or lose sight of the main objective.
   d. I can be counted on to contribute something original.
   e. I am always ready to back a good suggestion in the common interest.
   f. I am keen to look for the latest in new ideas and developments.
   g. I believe my capacity for cool judgement is appreciated by others.
   h. I can be relied upon to see that all essential work is organised.

IV. My characteristic approach to group work is that:
   a. I have a quiet interest in getting to know colleagues better.
   b. I am not reluctant to challenge the views of others or to hold a minority view myself.
   c. I can usually find a line of argument to refute unsound propositions.
   d. I think I have a talent for making things work once a plan has to be put into operation.
   e. I have a tendency to avoid the obvious and to come out with the unexpected.
   f. I bring a touch of perfectionism to any team job I undertake.
   g. I am ready to make use of contacts outside the group itself.
   h. While I am interested in all views I have no hesitation in making up my mind once a decision has to be made.

V. I gain satisfaction in a job because:
   a. I enjoy analysing situations and weighing up all the possible choices.
   b. I am interested in finding practical solutions to problems.
   c. I like to feel I am fostering good working relationships.
   d. I can have a strong influence on decisions.
   e. I can meet people who may have something new to offer.
   f. I can get people to agree on a necessary course of action.
   g. I feel in my element where I can give a task my full attention.
   h. I like to find a field that stretches my imagination.

VI. If I am suddenly given a difficult task with limited time and unfamiliar people:
   a. I would feel like retiring to a corner to devise a way out of the impasse before developing a line.
   b. I would be ready to work with the person who showed the most positive approach, however difficult he or she might be.
   c. I would find some way of reducing the size of the task by establishing what different individuals might best contribute.
   d. My natural sense of urgency would help to ensure that we did not fall behind schedule.

e. I believe I would keep cool and maintain my capacity to think straight.

f. I would retain a steadiness of purpose in spite of the pressures.

g. I would be prepared to take a positive lead if I felt the group was making no progress.

h. I would open up discussions with a view to stimulating new thoughts and getting something moving.

VII. With reference to the problems to which I am subject in working in groups.

a. I am apt to show my impatience with those who are obstructing progress.

b. Others may criticise me for being too analytical and insufficiently intuitive.

c. My desire to ensure that work is properly done can hold up proceedings.

d. I tend to get bored rather easily and rely on one or two stimulating members to spark me off.

e. I find it difficult to get started unless the goals are clear.

f. I am sometimes poor at explaining and clarifying complex points that occur to me.

g. I am conscious of demanding from others the things I cannot do myself.

h. I hesitate to get my points across when I run up against real opposition.

Team Role Inventory Analysis Sheet

Transpose the scores taken from pages 238–240, entering them section by section in the table below. Then add up the points in each column to give a total team role distribution score. The column headings relate to the various team role members described on pages 109–110.

Section	IMP	CO	SH	PL	RI	ME	TW	CF
I	g	d	f	c	a	h	b	e	
II	a	b	e	g	c	d	f	h	
III	h	a	c	d	f	g	e	b	
IV	d	h	b	e	g	c	a	f	
V	b	f	d	h	e	a	c	g	
VI	f	c	g	a	h	c	b	d	
VII	e	g	a	f	d	b	h	c	
Total								

APPENDIX B: REFERENCES

Audit Commission, 1994. *Seen but not Heard. Co-ordinating Community Child Health and Social Services for Children in Need*, HMSO, London.

Belbin, R.M., 1981. *Management Teams. Why they Succeed or Fail*, Butterworth Heinemann, Guildford.

Bone, M., 1977. *Pre-school Children and the Need for Daycare: OPCS Social Survey*, HMSO, London.

Clutterbuck, D., 1985. *Everyone Needs a Mentor*, Institute of Personnel Management, London.

Cohen, P., 1992. *A New Deal for Children? Implementation of the Children Act 1989 in the Counties*, Association of County Councils Publications, London.

Department of Health, 1993. *Children's Day Care Facilities at 31st March 1992*, HMSO, London.

Department of Health, 1989. *The Children Act 1989: Guidance and Regulations. Volume 2: Family support, day care and educational provision for young children*, HMSO, London.

Elfer, P., 1991. The Children Act and Day Care, *National Childrens Bureau Guidelines, No. 100*, London.

Fielder, F.E., 1971. Validation and Extension of the Contingency Model of Leadership Effectiveness, *Psychological Bulletin*, **76**, 128–48.

Handy, C., 1986. *Understanding Organisations*, Penguin, London.

Handy, C., 1992. *The Gods of Management*, Penguin, London.

Harrison, R., 1972. How to Describe your Organization, *Harvard Business Review*, Sept/Oct 1972.

Herzberg, F., 1966. *Work and the Nature of Man*, World Publishing Co., New York.

Herzberg, F., 1968. One More Time: How do you Motivate Employees?, *Harvard Business Review 46*.

Holmes, F. H. and Rahe, R. H., 1967. The Social Readjustment Rating Scale, *Journal of Psychomatic Research*, **11**, 213–18.

Jones, A. and Bitton, K., 1992. *The Future Shape of Children's Services*, National Childrens Bureau, London.

Levinson, Daniel J., 1978. *The Seasons of a Man's Life*, Ballantine Books, New York.

Maslow, A., 1954. *Motivation and Personality*, Harper and Row, New York.

Moss, P. and Pearce, A., 1995. *Valuing Quality in Early Childhood Services*, Paul Chapman, London.

National Childrens Bureau, 1994. *Young Children in Group Day Care: Guidelines for Good Practice*, NCB, London.

OPCS, 1995. *Daycare Services for Children*, HMSO, London.

Peters, T. and Waterman, R. H., 1982. *In search of Excellence*, Harper and Row, New York.

Pugh, G., 1988. *Services for Under Fives*, National Childrens Bureau, London.

Pugh, G., 1992. *Contemporary Issues in the Early Years*, Paul Chapman/National Childrens Bureau, London.

Pugh, G., 1993. *30 Years of Change for Children*, National Childrens Bureau, London.

Rosenthal, R. and Jacobson, L., 1968. *Pygmalion in the Classroom*, Holt, Rinehart and Winston, New York.

Rotter, J.B., 1966. Generalised Expectancies for Internal versus External Control of Reinforcement, *Psychological Monographs*, **30**, 1–26.

Rubin, Z. and McNeil, E.B., 1983. *The Psychology of Being Human*, Harper and Row, London.

Schaffer, R.H., 1990. *Making Decisions about Children: Psychological Questions and Answers*, Basil Blackwell, Oxford.

Selye, H., 1956. *The Stress of Life*, New York, McGraw Hill.

Smith, P., 1989. Overview of the Children Act 1989, *National Childrens Bureau Guidelines, No. 91*, London.

Thomas Coram Research Unit, 1994. *Implementing the Children Act for Children under Eight*, HMSO, London.

INDEX

evaluation of service *see* performance indicators
exclusion procedures   173
experiments   17, 18

Fielder, F. E.   39
filing systems   58–9
finance
    planning   59–60, 69, 180
    procedures   59, 179, 185
    reviewing processes   186
fire safety   10–11
food
    management policy   50, 168
    preparation procedures   174–5
Froebel, F.   73

General Adaptation Syndrome (GAS)   133–4
grievance procedures, staff   223

Handy, C.   13, 19, 23, 126
Harrison, Roger   19, 20
Hawthorne studies   31–2
Health and Safety at Work Act 1974   9
health and safety policy   50, 53, 153–4
heirarchy of needs, Maslow's   32–4
Herzberg's two-factor theory of motivation   34–5
hidden curriculum   78
homework   97, 210

ideology *see* cultures, organisational
illnesses   173
incentive theory (motivation)   29, 30
incident slips   61, 194
induction of new staff   106–7
interviews   105–6
    appraisal   121–2
    for new staff   104–6
    research   16
intimate care policy   55
intrinsic theory (motivation)   29, 30–1
invoices   185

job enhancement   35–6

language and literacy   79, 81, 89, 91
laundry room procedures   177
leadership   26, 38–43
learned helplessness   140
legislation   7–9, 10

see also Children Act 1989
Levinson, D. J.   142
life histories   16
locus of control theory (motivation)   35, 124

McKinsey's seven S's model   14–15
management theory *see* theories, management
managers
    good practice points   145–6
    job description   212–13
    skills required   232–7
marketing   63
Maslow's heirarchy of needs   32–4
mathematics   80, 89, 92, 97
matrix structure (organisations)   19, 21, 23–4
medication   57, 193–4
mentors and mentoring   107–8
mission statements   47–9, 150
models (management theory)   14, 18
Montessori, Maria   73–5
motivation   26–38

National Children's Bureau   8, 51, 54
National Occupational Standard Working With Young Children and their Families (NOSWWYCF)   118–19
Nurseries and Childminders Act 1948   9
nursery assistants   218
nursery nurses   216–17
NVQs (National Vocational Qualifications)   116, 117–19

observation   13, 16, 18, 32
open book management   37
open evenings   96
open questions   120–1
Organisation Consulting Group   69–70
organisational cultures   19–24, 46
organisational structures   18–20, 22–4
organisational theory   13–14, 17–18, 26

paradigms   14, 18
parents
    involvement in the curriculum   96–7
    and nursery as partners   2, 7, 50, 53, 88, 155–7, 183–4
    parent–child relationship   6, 88
    responsibilities   1–3, 45